101 Brain-Boosting Math Problems

By Lorraine Hopping Egan

SCHOLASTIC
PROFESSIONAL BOOKS

New York ⌐ Toronto ⌐ London ⌐ Auckland ⌐ Sydney ⌐ Mexico City ⌐ New Delhi ⌐ Hong Kong

Dedication

To Louise and Diane, with multiple thanks

Teachers may photocopy the reproducible pages in this book for classroom use. No other part of this publication may be reproduced in whole or in part, or stored in a retrieval system, or transmitted in any form or by any means, electronic, mechanical, photocopy, recording, or otherwise, without written permission of the publisher. For information regarding permission, write to Scholastic Inc., 555 Broadway, New York, NY 10012.

Cover design by Jaime Lucero

Cover Illustration by Michael Moran

Interior design by Ellen Matlach Hassell
for Boultinghouse & Boultinghouse, Inc.

Interior Illustration by Michael Moran and Manuel Rivera

ISBN: 0-590-37869-4

Copyright © 1999 by Lorraine Hopping Egan. All rights reserved.

Printed in the U.S.A.

Contents

Suggestions for Classroom Use 6

Chapter 1:
Numbers and Arithmetic

Terminator Math 7
(math terms)

Dial-a-Joke 1 8
(number code)

Dial-a-Joke 2 8
(number code)

Prime Target 9
(prime numbers; simple addition)

Clocking In 10
(simple addition; problem solving)

Age-Old Problem 10
(multiple-step problem solving)

Add Across 7-11 11
(simple addition)

Add Across Anything Goes 12
(simple addition)

Spotlight Addition 13
(addition; problem solving)

Unlucky Triangle 13
(addition; problem solving)

Tri-Corner Subtraction. 14
(subtraction; number patterns)

Turtle Number Race. 15
(divisibility; number patterns)

Hare Number Race. 16
(divisibility; number patterns)

Squared Off 17
(square numbers; number patterns)

Try for $25 18
(money addition)

Every Item $1. 19
(money addition)

Dollar Darts 20
(money addition)

Nuts! 21
(multiple-step problem solving)

4, 2, 1 . . . Contact!. 21
(mixed operations; number patterns)

Roman Square 22
(Roman numerals)

12 Angry Numbers 22
(addition; problem solving)

Funny Flowers 23
(number code; mixed operations)

Leaky Life Raft 24
(mental addition; problem solving)

Peak 48. 25
(mental addition)

The Windy 100. 26
(multiplication; factors)

The Windy 500 27
(multiplication; factors)

Product of the Times 1. 28
(multiplication)

Product of the Times 2. 29
(multiplication)

Product of the Times 3. 30
(multiplication)

Awe-Sum 45. 31
(addition; problem solving)

7 Up 31
(addition; problem solving)

9 Up 32
(mixed operations)

Shell Game 1 33
(mixed equations; algebraic thinking)

Shell Game 2 34
(mixed equations; algebraic thinking)

Shell Game 3 35
(mixed equations; algebraic thinking)

Fruit Bowl 1 36
(problem solving)

Fruit Bowl 2 37
(problem solving)

6-Digit Scramble 1 37
(divisibility formulas)

6-Digit Scramble 2 38
(divisibility formulas)

7-Digit Scramble 38
(divisibility formulas)

Dates and Places 39
(place value; problem solving)

Number Circle 1 40
(mixed math)

Number Circle 2 41
(mixed math)

Gearing Up 42
(ratios; division)

E.S.P. Number 43
(four-digit subtraction)

Chapter 2:
Geometry and Coordinates

Pot of Gold 1 44
(coordinates; compass directions)

Pot of Gold 2 45
(coordinates; compass directions)

Escape from Antcatraz 46
(coordinates; compass directions)

Gem Tones 1 47
(spatial thinking; symmetry)

Gem Tones 2 47
(spatial thinking; symmetry)

Gem Tones 3 48
(spatial thinking; symmetry)

3-D Cube 48
(two- and three-dimensional polygons)

Dream House 49
(topology)

Letter Letter 49
(symmetry)

Six Ugly Bugs 50
(spatial relations)

Creepy Crawly Corral 51
(two-dimensional shapes;
spatial relations)

Sheepish Grid 52
(topology)

Fats Domino 53
(spatial relations; number patterns)

Paper Door 54
(topology)

Smell the Roses 55
(three-dimensional polygons;
spatial relations)

Boxed In 56
(spatial relations; three-dimensional
thinking)

5 to 1 57
(two-dimensional shapes)

Chip off the Old Block 1 58
(two-dimensional shapes)

Chip off the Old Block 2 59
(two-dimensional shapes)

Chip off the Old Block 3 59
(two-dimensional shapes)

Triangle Triangle 60
(two-dimensional shapes)

Triangle Square 60
(two-dimensional shapes)

Triangle Circle 61
(two-dimensional shapes)

Circle 10 62
   (two-dimensional shapes)

Shell-Shocked 63
   (two-dimensional shapes; problem solving)

Checkered Past 1 64
   (two-dimensional shapes; spatial relations)

Checkered Past 2 65
   (two-dimensional shapes; spatial relations)

Even Stevens 66
   (two-dimensional shapes; spatial relations)

Balanced Valance 67
   (two-dimensional shapes; spatial relations)

Mirror Match-Up 68
   (symmetry; problem solving)

Victor's Vector 69
   (coordinate grids; space-time-distance
   formula)

Chapter 3:
Logical Thinking

31 Up 70
   (number patterns)

Strange Range 70
   (number patterns)

Area Code Explosion 71
   (number patterns; codes)

Zip Code Geography 71
   (number patterns; codes)

Secrets of the Interstates—Unlocked! 72
   (number patterns; codes)

Year to Year 72
   (palindromes; number patterns)

Time Line 73
   (visual patterns)

Search in Vain 73
   (letter and number patterns)

Victor's Victory 1 74
   (geometric patterns)

Victor's Victory 2 75
   (geometric patterns)

Klepto Cat 76
   (attributes; logical thinking)

Klepto Cat Returns 76
   (attributes; logical thinking)

Son of Klepto Cat 77
   (attributes; logical thinking)

Triple Play 1 77
   (number patterns; multiplication of
   large numbers)

Triple Play 2 78
   (number patterns; multiplication of
   large numbers)

Triple Play 3 78
   (number patterns; multiplication of
   large numbers)

Cats and Fleas 79
   (problem solving)

Gopher It 1 80
   (logical thinking; problem solving)

Gopher It 2 81
   (logical thinking; problem solving)

Gopher It 3 82
   (logical thinking; problem solving)

Mixed Message 1 83
   (letter patterns; logical thinking)

Mixed Message 2 84
   (letter patterns; logical thinking)

Figure It (Out) Skaters 85
   (logical thinking)

Siberian Tiger 1 86
   (logical thinking; spatial relations)

Siberian Tiger 2 87
   (logical thinking; spatial relations)

Beastie Balance 88
   (algebraic thinking)

Answers 89

Suggestions for Classroom Use

Among the 101 math puzzles in this book, you'll find fun versions of the most popular classics as well as many new puzzles that will challenge your students. In general, the easier puzzles are presented at the beginning of each chapter. In a few cases, increasingly challenging versions of a puzzle are grouped together.

Each puzzle includes simple directions, an example (where appropriate), **Think About It!** suggestions that encourage students to try various strategies, and a **Big Fat Hint** in case students get stuck. Answers to the puzzles appear in the back of the book. Begin by presenting the puzzles to students without the **Big Fat Hint** (and without the answer, of course). Provide the hint only after students have thoroughly considered the ideas in the **Think About It!** section and are still stumped.

Here are a few suggestions for integrating the puzzles into your daily classroom routine:

Bulletin Board Stumpers

Post a puzzle each morning and challenge students to solve it by the end of the day. Encourage them to work together, share strategies, and compare solutions.

Early Birds and Last-to-Leave

Hand out puzzles to students who finish their work first, arrive to class early, or must wait around at the end of the day.

Puzzle Contest

Divide students into groups of three or four and give each group the same stack of five to ten puzzles. Groups can divide the puzzles among members or work cooperatively. Which group can solve the puzzles first?

Copycat Puzzle Makers

Challenge students to solve a puzzle and then create a new, similar puzzle for others to solve. Compile the puzzles in a notebook for future classroom use.

Classroom Privileges

Allow students to trade three solved puzzles for a classroom privilege, such as being first in line for lunch.

One for All

Throughout the school year, have students solve the puzzles at home or in their free time. Each time students complete a puzzle, they exchange it for the next one in the book. The goal is to earn a reward by completing all 101 puzzles by the end of the year.

All for One

To jump-start the brain cells, present the class with a puzzle at the beginning of the school day and work together to solve it. Encourage a variety of strategies, whenever appropriate.

Make Up Time

When two students argue or fight, give them a math puzzle to solve together—not as punishment, of course, but as a way to encourage them to work cooperatively.

Name _____   Date _____

Terminator Math

The solutions for these three puzzles are math terms. The first one is "round up"—get it? (Round up to the nearest ten or hundred, and so on.) Can you figure out the other two?

ZZZZZZZ   TИUOƆ

1. _____   2. _____   3. _____

THINK ABOUT IT!

⤷ As you look at the puzzles, say aloud any words that come to mind.

⤷ Think of homonyms—two words that sound the same but have different meanings, such as *whole* and *hole*.

⤷ Think of words that have more than one meaning. For instance, the word *round* can mean "round like a circle" or "to round a number."

Make up your own Terminator Math puzzle. Use one of the math words from the box.

triangle	long division	times table
multiply	number line	square root

Dial-a-Joke 1

On a telephone, each of the numbers 2 through 9 stands for three different letters. Read the joke below. Then substitute letters for numbers to decode the punch line.

Telephone Letter Code

Caller: Why doesn't the *X* work on this phone?

Operator: __ __ __   __ __ __ __ __
8 4 3   5 4 6 3 7

__ __ __   __ __ __ __ __ __ __ .
2 7 3   2 7 6 7 7 3 3

THINK ABOUT IT!

Each word has at least one vowel. The words form a sentence. How can you use these facts to solve the puzzle?

BIG FAT HINT The second word is *lines.*

Dial-a-Joke 2

Use the Telephone Letter Code to decode the punch line.

Telephone Letter Code

Caller: I'd like to call someone in Alaska.

Operator: __ __ __ __ __ __   __ __ __ ?
5 8 6 3 2 8   9 4 6

THINK ABOUT IT!

How can you organize the code into a table to test all the possible letters?

BIG FAT HINT The answer includes the name of a city in Alaska that starts with the letter *J.*

101 Brain-Boosting Math Puzzles   Scholastic Professional Books

Name _____ Date _____

Prime Target

Do you recognize these numbers: 2, 3, 5, 7, 11, 13, and so on? These are *prime numbers*. They are evenly divisible by only two numbers, 1 and themselves. One unproven math rule says that you can get any even number by adding two prime numbers. Do you believe it?

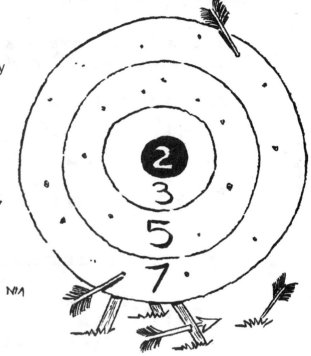

Which two prime numbers, when added, equal these even numbers? **Remember that 1 is *not* a prime number.**

1. _____ + _____ = 4

2. _____ + _____ = 6

3. _____ + _____ = 10

4. _____ + _____ = 12

5. _____ + _____ = 18

6. _____ + _____ = 24

THINK ABOUT IT!

⤷ Is there more than one answer for some numbers?

⤷ **Careful!** Not all odd numbers are prime!

BIG FAT HINT! Try dividing the number in half. If the result is an odd number, it may be prime. If the result is even (other than 2), which is prime), keep adding 1 and subtracting 1 to find two odd (and possibly prime) numbers. **Example: 12 ÷ 2 = 6** The result is even, so add 1 (6 + 1 = 7) and subtract 1 (6 − 1 = 5) to get 7 + 5. This trick doesn't always work, but it's a shortcut for some numbers.

101 Brain-Boosting Math Puzzles Scholastic Professional Books

Clocking In

At what time do the digits of a digital clock have the greatest sum? Fill in the digits on the clock. Write the sum of the digits in the box at right.

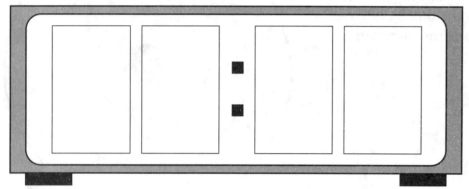 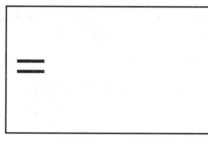

THINK ABOUT IT!

↳ What are all the possible digits for the hours?

↳ What are all the possible digits for the minutes?

BIG FAT HINT The answer is not 12:59 (1 + 2 + 5 + 9 = 17).

Age-Old Problem

Suppose you are five times older than your cousin. In two years, you will be three times older. Four years after that, you will be twice as old. What are the current ages of you and your cousin?

Your age: _____ **Your cousin's age:** _____

THINK ABOUT IT!

One strategy to use is guess and check. Plug in numbers for the current ages of you and your cousin. Then see if these numbers work with the rest of the problem.

BIG FAT HINT Five years after you are twice as old, your cousin will be a teenager. You will then be an adult.

101 Brain-Boosting Math Puzzles   Scholastic Professional Books

Add Across 7-11

An Add Across works like a crossword puzzle, except with numbers. Each row or column of digits adds up to either 7 or 11. The number in the margin tells you the sum.

Example: The digits of the first down answer add up to 7 (5 + 2).

Here are two more rules:

↳ There are no zeros in the crossword puzzle.

↳ No digit appears more than once in the same answer. For example, you couldn't use the numbers 3, 5, and 3 (3 + 5 + 3 = 11) because there are two 3's.

THINK ABOUT IT!

↳ What other numbers, besides 5 and 2 (5 + 2), add up to 7?

↳ What are three different numbers that add up to 7? To 11?

↳ What are the only four different numbers that add up to 11?

101 Brain-Boosting Math Puzzles   Scholastic Professional Books

Name _____ Date _____

Add Across Anything Goes

An Add Across works like a crossword puzzle, except with numbers.
The digits in each row or column add up to the sum in the margin.

Example: The digits in the first across answer add up to 18 (9 + 8 + 1).

Here are two more rules:

↳ There are no zeros in the puzzle.

↳ No digit appears more than
once in the same answer.
For example, you couldn't
use 2 and 2 (2 + 2 = 4)
because it has two 2's.

	15↓	18↓	17↓		11↓	8↓	
18→	9	8	1				←4
18→							←7
17→							
11→							
11→							
7→							←17
13→				2	9	7	←18
	↑10	↑12		↑15	↑20	↑15	

THINK ABOUT IT!

↳ An odd number plus an even number equals an odd number (8 + 7 = 15).

↳ Adding either two even numbers (6 + 4 = 10) or two odd numbers (3 + 7 = 10)
equals an even number.

↳ What are the only two different numbers that add up to 4?

↳ What two numbers add up to 7?

↳ What five numbers add up to 15?

BIG FAT HINT • The number in the center of the puzzle is 65.
• Three numbers that add up to 20 are 5, 6, and 9.

101 Brain-Boosting Math Puzzles Scholastic Professional Books

Name _____ Date _____

Spotlight Addition

Each spotlight (circle) has a certain brightness between 1 and 15. Figure out how bright each spotlight is by following these rules:

↪ The number in the center where all three spotlights meet is 28. This is the sum of the three spotlight values.

↪ The number where spotlight A and spotlight B overlap is 22. This is the sum of the values of spotlight A and B.

↪ The number where spotlight B and spotlight C overlap is 14. This is the sum of the values of spotlight B and C.

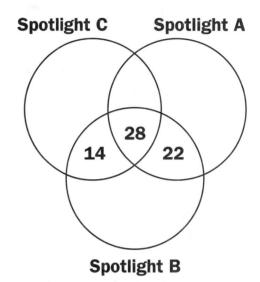

Spotlight C   **Spotlight A**

14   28   22

Spotlight B

THINK ABOUT IT!

↪ Which spotlight has the highest value? Which has the lowest value?

↪ How can you tell that all three numbers are not the same?

BIG FAT HINT
• The number 28 is not evenly divisible by 3.
• If two numbers add up to an even number, both numbers must be either odd or even.

Name _____ Date _____

Unlucky Triangle

Put the numbers 0 through 8 in the nine circles on the triangle.

Here are the rules:

↪ Each side of the triangle must add up to unlucky 13.

↪ Use each digit only once.

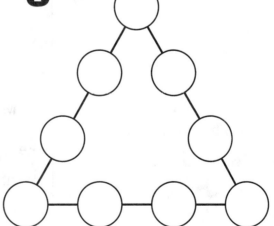

Number List
0
1
2
3
4
5
6
7
8

THINK ABOUT IT!

↪ What four different digits add up to 13? Is there more than one combination?

↪ Is it better to put the higher numbers at the corners or on the sides?

BIG FAT HINT The numbers 0, 1, and 2 go at each of the three corners.

101 Brain-Boosting Math Puzzles   Scholastic Professional Books

Tri-Corner Subtraction

A tri-corner hat has three corners. This tri-corner hat has a number at each corner.

Here's a larger, upside-down tri-corner hat around the first hat. The numbers at each of its corners are the differences between the numbers on the first hat.

Example: At the top left corner, 5 − 3 = 2. At the bottom corner, 7 − 5 = 2. In the top right corner, 7 − 3 = 4.

Here's a larger tri-corner hat, right side up again, around the first two hats.

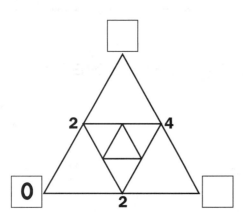

What are the numbers at its corners? Subtract the numbers of the second hat to find out.

Example: At bottom left corner, 2 − 2 = 0.

Fill in the other two numbers. Remember these three numbers.

Start a new tri-corner hat puzzle. Write any three numbers at the corners.

Draw a larger, upside-down hat outside the first hat. Subtract to find the numbers. Keep drawing hats until you see a pattern.

What is the pattern?

_____

THINK ABOUT IT!

↳ Make several tri-corner hat puzzles, using new numbers each time.

BIG FAT HINT You might need more than three tri-corner hats to see the pattern.

101 Brain-Boosting Math Puzzles Scholastic Professional Books

Turtle Number Race

Which three turtles will reach the winner's circle? Each turtle must run the race according to the track rules. For example, Turtle 1 must race along the "odd" track because it is an odd number. It must then take the "not divisible by 3" track. Where will the other turtles end up?

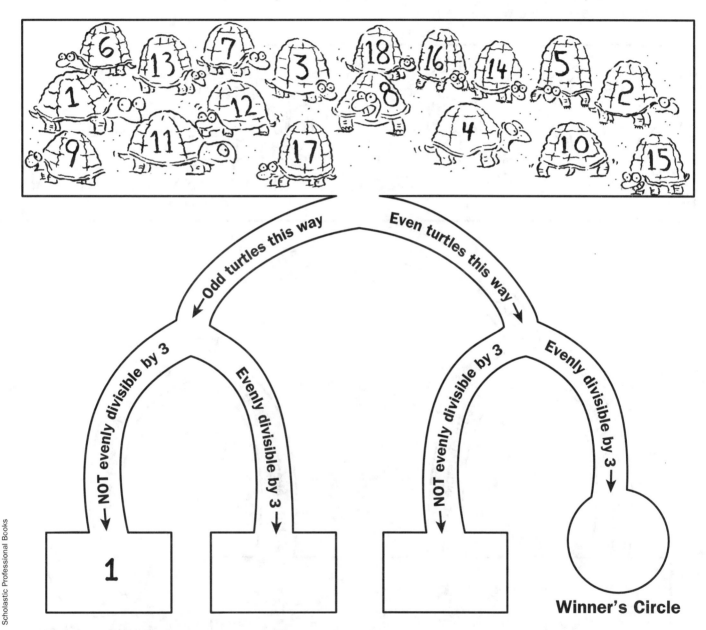

Winner's Circle

THINK ABOUT IT!

⤷ Before you start, look at the group of numbers. Which numbers do you predict will win? Why?

⤷ Where will the odd prime numbers (3, 5, 7, 11, and so on) end up?

⤷ Where will the only even prime number (2) end up?

BIG FAT HINT The three winners are all divisible by 3 and 2. They are also divisible by 6.

101 Brain-Boosting Math Puzzles Scholastic Professional Books

Name _____ Date _____

Hare Number Race

Which two hares will reach the winner's circle? Each hare must run the race according to the properties of its number. For example, Hare 5 must race along the "odd" track because it is odd. It must then take the "divisible by 5" track, which doesn't lead to the winner's circle.

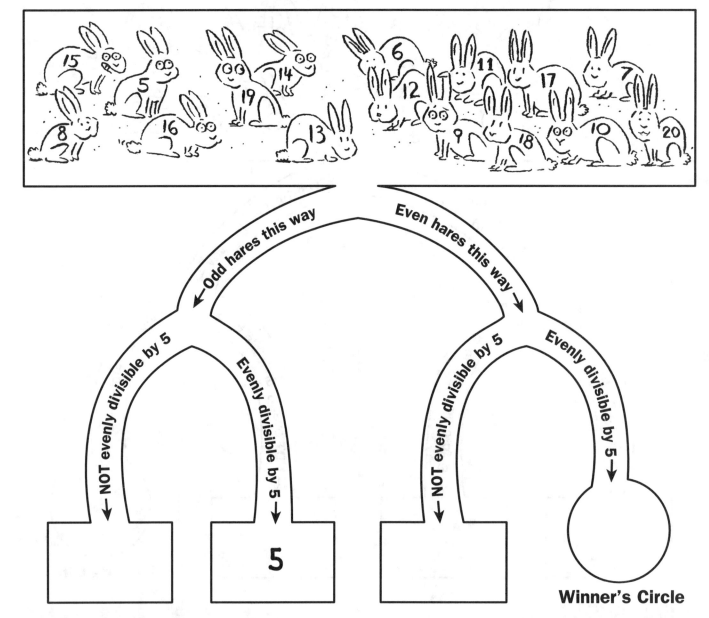

THINK ABOUT IT!

↳ Before you test each number, which numbers do you predict will win? Why?

↳ Which other hares will join number 5?

101 Brain-Boosting Math Puzzles   Scholastic Professional Books

BIG FAT HINT The two winners are divisible by 5 and 2 (because they're even).

Squared Off

Multiply a number by itself and you get a square ($6 \times 6 = 36$). Here's a way to figure out squares by adding.

1. The black dot stands for 1. The number 1 is a square ($1 \times 1 = 1$).

2. Color the 3 circles around the black dot: $1 + 3 = 4$. The number 4 is a square, too ($2 \times 2 = 4$).

3. Color the next 5 circles that are nearest to the colored dots. How many dots in all are colored now? $1 + 3 + 5 = $ _____. (Hint: It's the next square—3×3!)

4. Keep coloring the dots that are nearest to the colored dots. Then add the colored dots to find these squares:

$1 + 3 + 5 + 7 = $ _____

$1 + 3 + 5 + 7 + 9 = $ _____

$1 + 3 + 5 + 7 + 9 + 11 = $ _____

$1 + 3 + 5 + 7 + 9 + 11 + 13 = $ _____

$1 + 3 + 5 + 7 + 9 + 11 + 13 + 15 = $ _____

$1 + 3 + 5 + 7 + 9 + 11 + 13 + 15 + 17 = $ _____

$1 + 3 + 5 + 7 + 9 + 11 + 13 + 15 + 17 + 19 = $ _____

THINK ABOUT IT!

Can you spot the pattern?

Try for $25

Lucky you! You've won a $25 gift certificate. There's a hitch. You must spend every penny of it on three different items. Here's what's for sale:

List three items you can buy.

1. _____

2. _____

3. _____

THINK ABOUT IT!

↳ Which numbers can you eliminate (rule out) right away?

↳ Can you buy four items worth exactly $25? List them below.

1. _____

2. _____

3. _____

4. _____

BIG FAT HINT Cross off the items that cost $20 and $23. They're too large to include in this three-number problem.

101 Brain-Boosting Math Puzzles   Scholastic Professional Books

Name _____ Date _____

Every Item $1

A penny, a nickel, a dime, and quarter equal 41 cents. Using combinations of these coins only, can you figure out combinations that equal $1 exactly? The example shows the answer for 6 coins.

	Pennies	Nickels	Dimes	Quarters	Equation
6 coins	0	1	2	3	5¢ + 20¢ + 75¢ = $1
12 coins					
16 coins					
50 coins					

THINK ABOUT IT!

↳ What's the least number of coins needed to make $1?

↳ Guess and check is one way to solve this problem. Can you find a faster strategy?

↳ The number of coins increases with each problem. How should the value of the coins change?

↳ There's more than one answer for each problem. How many answers can you find?

BIG FAT HINT For 50 coins, most of the coins have to be pennies. The number of pennies must be evenly divisible by 5 in order to reach an even $1. Do you see why?

101 Brain-Boosting Math Puzzles   Scholastic Professional Books

Name _____ Date _____

Dollar Darts

Can you score exactly $100 on this Dollar Dart board
without hitting the bull's-eye? Here's how many darts
you can use for each turn. Write the number you
would need to hit on each turn.

2 Darts	
3 Darts	
4 Darts	
5 Darts	
6 Darts	
7 Darts	

THINK ABOUT IT!

⤷ Solve the first three problems. Then look for a pattern that makes
solving the rest of the problems easier.

⤷ There is more than one way to complete the last two problems.
How many ways can you find?

BIG FAT HINT Break down an amount from the previous
problem into two equal amounts. **Example:** Divide $10 into $5 and $5.

101 Brain-Boosting Math Puzzles   Scholastic Professional Books

Nuts!

Abby Squirrel found a pile of nuts. She ate 2 nuts and then took half of what was left to eat later.

Billy Squirrel found the pile next. Like Abby, he ate 2 nuts and took half of what was left to eat later.

Curly Squirrel finally found the pile. He ate all 15 nuts in one sitting.

Which squirrel ate twice as many nuts as which other squirrel?

_____

	nuts eaten	nuts taken
Curly Squirrel	**15**	
Billy Squirrel		
Abby Squirrel		

THINK ABOUT IT!
Work backward, starting with Curly's 15 nuts.

BIG FAT HINT *Twice as much* (multiplying by 2) is the opposite of *half as much* (dividing by 2).

4, 2, 1...Contact!

Pick a number—any number. Follow these rules:

↳ If it's even, divide it by 2.

↳ If it's odd, multiply by 3 and add 1.

Each time you get an answer, follow the rules again. Keep going until you see a pattern. Be very patient! With some numbers, it may take many steps to see the pattern.

Example: Take the number 12. Here's what happens:

$$12 \div 2 = 6$$
$$6 \div 2 = 3$$
$$3 \times 3 = 9; 9 + 1 = 10$$
$$10 \div 2 = 5$$
$$5 \times 3 = 15; 15 + 1 = 16$$
$$16 \div 2 = 8$$

THINK ABOUT IT!
Finish the pattern for the number 12. Then pick a new number. Choose a smaller number the first time. Then try a larger number. You may use a calculator.

101 Brain-Boosting Math Puzzles   Scholastic Professional Books

Name _____ Date _____

Roman Square

This puzzle works like a crossword puzzle, except it uses Roman numerals.

Change the numbers in the clues to Roman numerals. Then write the Roman numerals in the grid.

	a	b	c	d
e				
f				
g				

Across

a. 1,300

e. 145

f. 17

g. 13

Down

a. 1,120

b. 116

c. 152

d. 107

THINK ABOUT IT!

↳ Do the easy clues, such as f and g, first. Then use the letters to help you solve the harder clues.

↳ List the Roman numerals in order of value, starting with M (1,000).

BIG FAT HINT

M = 1,000	C = 100
L = 50	X = 10
V = 5	I = 1

Name _____ Date _____

12 Angry Numbers

The numbers 1 through 12 are really angry! No two consecutive numbers want to be next to each other. Can you help them?

Write the numbers in the circles so that no line connects two consecutive numbers.

Example: 3 *cannot* be connected by a line to 2 or 4.

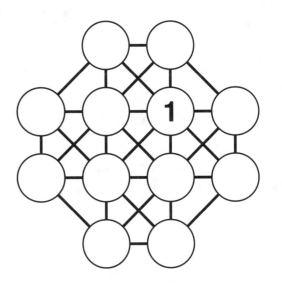

THINK ABOUT IT!

What numbers, besides 1, should go in the four center circles?

BIG FAT HINT Try making all four center numbers odd.

101 Brain-Boosting Math Puzzles Scholastic Professional Books

Funny Flowers

To find the funny flower punch line, solve the problems below. Read the clues. Substitute the numbers for the letters, and add, subtract, multiply, or divide. Then change the number to a letter. The letters in the last column will spell out the punch line to the joke.

Number Codes

10	3	11	5	9	7	2	8
E	I	L	N	O	S	T	V

What did the daisies protest against?

Clues	Number	Letter
1. Subtract I from L.	11 – 3 = 8	8 = V
2. Divide O by I.		
3. Multiply I by I.		
4. The greatest number		
5. Multiply N by T.		
6. Divide E by N.		
7. Subtract T from O.		
8. Add S and T.		
9. Subtract I from V.		
10. Subtract O from L.		
11. Add I and N.		

Punch Line ↑

THINK ABOUT IT!

Can you guess the punch line before you solve all the clues?

101 Brain-Boosting Math Puzzles   Scholastic Professional Books

Leaky Life Raft

You're stuck at sea on a leaky raft with 9 important items. Can you place the items evenly so that the raft doesn't tip over? The total weight of the items in each row, column, or diagonal must add up to 21. Put one item in each square. (The cheese wheel weighing 7 units goes in the middle square.)

Important Item	Weight
Picture of Mom	3 units
Foot-long sandwich	4 units
Fuzzy sweater	5 units
Bucket of golf balls	6 units
Cheese wheel	7 units
Math puzzle books	8 units
Cowboy boots	9 units
Giant jar of pickles	10 units
Tabby cat	11 units

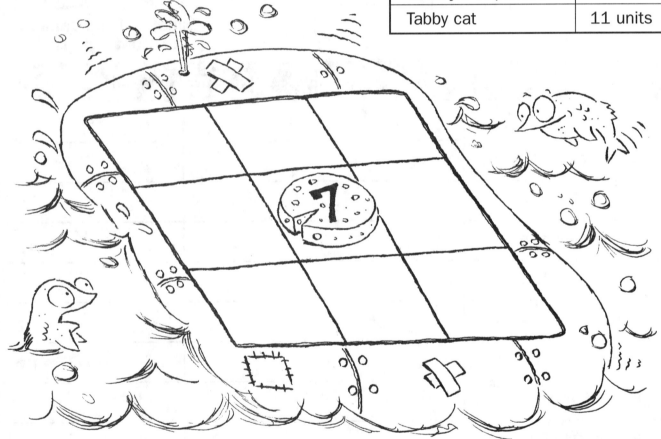

THINK ABOUT IT!

↳ Start by completing the row, column, and diagonals that include the number 7 in the middle square.

↳ The target number is 21. What is 21 − 7? Of the numbers on the list, which numbers total that amount?

↳ What are the lightest and heaviest items?

BIG FAT HINT Put the lightest item and the heaviest item in the middle column.

101 Brain-Boosting Math Puzzles   Scholastic Professional Books

Peak 48

Place the even numbers 2 through 24 on the mountain trails.

Here are the rules:

↳ Use each number only once.

↳ The numbers on each of the six trails must add up to 48.
  (Three trails have four numbers. Three trails have three numbers.)

↳ Always start from a square at the bottom of the mountain.

↳ You cannot backtrack down the mountain.

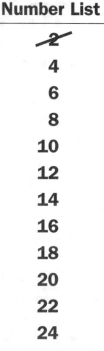

Number List
~~2~~
4
6
8
10
12
14
16
18
20
22
24

48

2

THINK ABOUT IT!

↳ Find each of the six trails. Which trails need larger numbers to total 48?

↳ Which trails need smaller numbers?

↳ Cross off numbers on the list as you use them.

101 Brain-Boosting Math Puzzles Scholastic Professional Books

Name _____ Date _____

The Windy 100

Hot-air balloons depend on the wind to carry them. In this race, the numbers in the winning path, when multiplied, equal 100. Can you find the correct path?

↳ Start at the top with the number 2.

↳ Float along the lines to the bottom, multiplying the numbers as you go. Each path has 5 numbers you must multiply.

↳ You *cannot* go backward (up) or sideways. You can move diagonally.

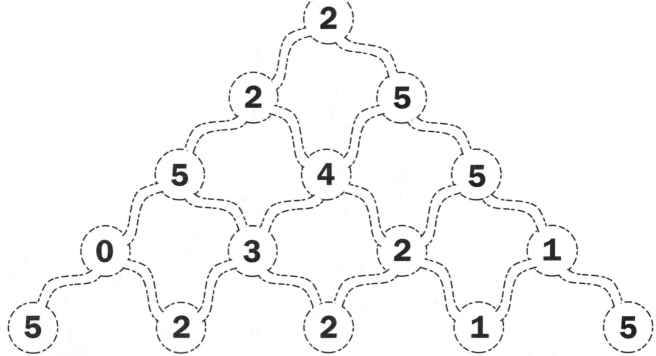

THINK ABOUT IT!

↳ Which path can you quickly rule out?

↳ What are the factors of 100?

BIG FAT HINT Some of the factors of 100 are 1, 2, 4, 5, 10 (2 × 5), and 25 (5 × 5).

101 Brain-Boosting Math Puzzles Scholastic Professional Books

The Windy 500

In this windy hot-air balloon race, float down the paths and multiply the numbers as you go. The numbers in the winning path equal 500. Can you find it?

↳ Start at the top with the number 2.

↳ Follow the lines, always moving down. Don't go backward (up) or sideways.

↳ Each path has five numbers you must multiply.

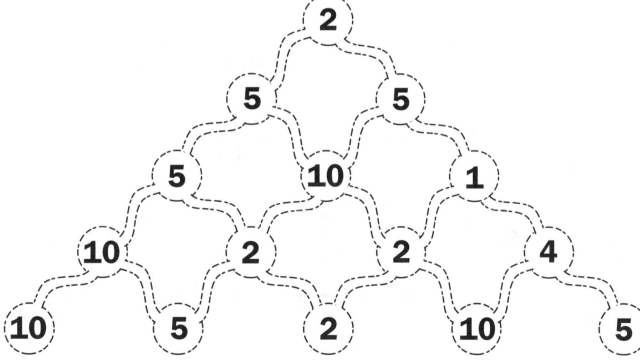

THINK ABOUT IT!

What are the factors of 500? Start with 100 × 5. Then break down 100 into its factors.

BIG FAT HINT Remember—some of the factors of 100 are 1, 2, 4, 5, 10 (2 × 5), and 25 (5 × 5).

101 Brain-Boosting Math Puzzles Scholastic Professional Books

Product of the Times 1

Place the numbers 1 through 8 in the grid. Sound easy? Here's the trick:

↳ Put only two numbers in each row and column.

↳ When multiplied, the two numbers must equal the product in the margin.

Example: The first row must have two numbers that equal a product of 24. The numbers could be either 8 × 3 or 6 × 4. They could go in any two of the four boxes in the row. It's up to you to make all the numbers fit.

				24
				4
				12
				35
8	**10**	**12**	**42**	

Number List
1
2
3
4
5
6
7
8

THINK ABOUT IT!

↳ What are the factors of each product?

↳ What are the only factors of 35 (besides 1 and 35)?

↳ What numbers have only two possible factors from 1 through 8?

BIG FAT HINT The number 8 goes in the first row and the first column.

101 Brain-Boosting Math Puzzles Scholastic Professional Books

Product of the Times 2

Place the numbers 2 through 9 in the grid. Here are the rules:

↳ Use each number only once.

↳ Put only two numbers in each row and column.

↳ When multiplied, the two numbers must equal the product in the margin.

Example: The numbers in the first row equal a product of 14. The only two possible numbers are 2 and 7 (2 × 7 = 14). The numbers could go in any two of the four boxes in the row.

				14
				18
				32
				45
12	24	36	35	

Number List
2
3
4
5
6
7
8
9

THINK ABOUT IT!

What are the factors of each of product?

BIG FAT HINT The first number in the grid is 2.

Name _____ Date _____

Product of the Times 3

Place the numbers 2 through 9 in the grid. Here are the rules:

↳ Use each number only once.

↳ Put only two numbers in each row and column.

↳ When multiplied, the two numbers equal the product in the margin.

Example: The two numbers in the first row equal a product of 12.

				12
				36
				56
				15
18	**20**	**24**	**42**	

Number List

2
3
4
5
6
7
8
9

THINK ABOUT IT!

↳ What are the factors of each product?

↳ The numbers along the diagonal equal a product of 64.
   What different numbers from 2 through 9 equal a product of 64?

BIG FAT HINT The first number in the grid is 2.

101 Brain-Boosting Math Puzzles   Scholastic Professional Books

Awe-Sum 45

The number 45 is truly awesome. To get 45, you can add $1 + 2 + 3 + 4 + 5 + 6 + 7 + 8 + 9$. (Try it!) You can also add other consecutive numbers to get 45.

Find four ways to make a sum of 45 with consecutive numbers.

2 numbers: _____ + _____ = **45**

3 numbers: _____ + _____ + _____ = **45**

5 numbers: _____ + _____ + _____ + _____ + _____ = **45**

6 numbers: _____ + _____ + _____ + _____ + _____ + _____ = **45**

THINK ABOUT IT!

↪ Every odd number greater than 1 is the sum of two consecutive numbers, for example, $6 + 7 = 13$. How can you use this fact to solve part of the Awe-Sum 45 problem?

↪ Will the numbers in the three-number equation be greater or less than the numbers in the two-number equation?

BIG FAT HINT The starting number for each equation decreases in order. The first number in the two-number equation is 22.

---

7 Up

Put the numbers 1 through 7 in the circles. In each triangle, two of the numbers must add up to the third number.

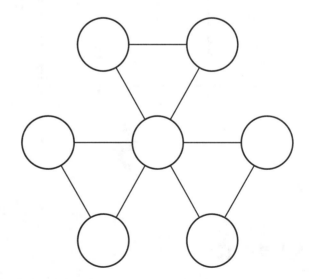

THINK ABOUT IT!

↪ What number should go in the center?

↪ What number should be the key sum (the one that the other two numbers add up to)?

Numbers and Arithmetic

101 Brain-Boosting Math Puzzles   Scholastic Professional Books

Name _____ Date _____

9 Up

The numbers 1 through 9 belong in the nine boxes below. Where does each number belong? Use the clues to help you find the right spots.

Number List
1 2 3 4 5 6 7 8 ~~9~~

Consecutive numbers out of order	The sum of these numbers equals 17	Subtract two numbers to get the third number	
			Three even numbers in order
			Consecutive numbers in reverse order
	9		**Three odd numbers that add up to 21**

THINK ABOUT IT!

↳ No single clue reveals an answer. For each clue, write all the possible numbers in the squares. Then use the other clues to rule out numbers. Remember: Use each digit only once.

↳ Stuck? Start in the middle instead of the top.

101 Brain-Boosting Math Puzzles Scholastic Professional Books

BIG FAT HINT The first digit is 4.

Name _____   Date _____

Shell Game 1

Each type of shell is worth a different value. The values are all single digits (0–9).
Study the equations to figure out the value of each shell. Write the values under each shell.

1.  × [shell] = [shell]

   | 2 | × | [ ] | = | [ ] |

2. [shell] + [shell] = [shell]

   | [ ] | + | [ ] | = | [ ] |

3. [shell] − [shell] = [shell] + 1

   | [ ] | − | [ ] | = | [ ] | + 1

4. [shell] ÷ [shell] = [shell]

   | [ ] | ÷ | [ ] | = | [ ] |

[shell] = [ ]

[shell] = [ ]

[shell] = [ ]

THINK ABOUT IT!

☞ Using the guess and check strategy is one way to solve this
  problem. Plug in numbers and see which ones fit.

☞ Which shell has the greatest value? Which shell has the least
  value? Can you put the shells in order from greatest to least?

BIG FAT HINT • The first problem is a multiplication problem. List all the factors of 4, 6, 8, and 9.
• Which numbers fit all the equations?

101 Brain-Boosting Math Puzzles Scholastic Professional Books

Name _____ Date _____

Shell Game 2

Each type of shell is worth a different value. Study
the equations to figure out what each shell is worth.

1.   × [   ] = [   ]

    [   ] × [   ] = [   ]

2. [   ] ÷ [   ] = [   ]

    [   ] ÷ [   ] = [   ]

3.  − =  + **6**

    [   ] − [   ] = [   ] + **6**

4.  + =

    [   ] + [   ] = **12**

THINK ABOUT IT!

↳ Using the guess and check strategy is one way to solve this problem.
   Plug in numbers and see which ones fit.

↳ How can you narrow down the choices? Can you put the shells in order
   from least to greatest without knowing their exact values?

101 Brain-Boosting Math Puzzles Scholastic Professional Books

BIG FAT HINT The highest value of a shell is 12.

Name _____ Date _____

Shell Game 3

The value of each type of shell is different. How much is each shell worth?

1.

| 2 | × | 9 | = | | × | |

2.

| | × | | = | | × | | × | |

3.

| | = | | + | | + | |

4.

| | − | | = | |

5.

| | = | | × | |

6.

| | × | | = | | − | |

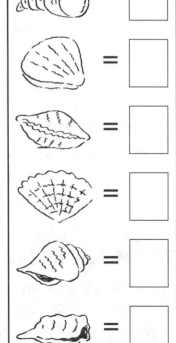

THINK ABOUT IT!

↪ See if you can order the shells from least to greatest.

101 Brain-Boosting Math Puzzles   Scholastic Professional Books

Name _____ Date _____

Fruit Bowl 1

Look at the scales to figure out the answers to these weighty questions.

A.

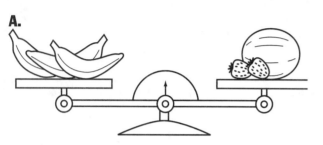

3 bananas = 2 strawberries + 1 melon

B.

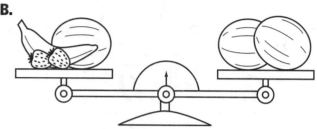

2 strawberries + 1 melon + 1 banana = 2 melons

C.

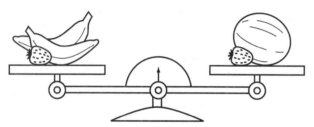

1 strawberry + 2 bananas = 1 melon + 1 strawberry

D.

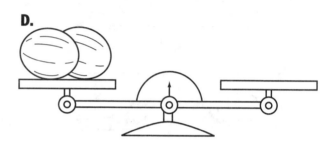

2 melons = what 6 fruits?

1. Which fruit weighs the most? List the fruits from heaviest to lightest:

_____

_____

_____

2. The banana weighs 2 units. How many units do the other fruits weigh?

1 strawberry = _____ **unit or units**   **1 melon =** _____ **unit or units**

3. One side of the Scale D has 2 melons.
Which six fruits would you use to balance the other side?

_____

THINK ABOUT IT!

⤷ Simplify the problem. For example, cross out the strawberries
  on Scale C. Now 2 bananas = 1 melon.

⤷ Which fruit weighs twice as much as the strawberry?

⤷ Which fruit weighs twice as much as the banana?

BIG FAT HINT
• Cross out 1 strawberry from each side of the third balance.
• Plug in 2 units for the bananas. Then try plugging in other
  numbers for the strawberry and melon. Which numbers work?

101 Brain-Boosting Math Puzzles   Scholastic Professional Books

Fruit Bowl 2

How many units does each fruit weigh?
(Each one has a different weight.)

cherry + cherry + pear = 10 units

cherry + apple + pear = 12 units

cherry + pear + pear = 11 units

1 cherry = _____ **units**

1 pear = _____ **units**

1 apple = _____ **units**

THINK ABOUT IT!

↳ The middle equation is the only one with all three kinds of fruit.

↳ What three different numbers, when added, equal 12? Make a list.

BIG FAT HINT The three
weights are consecutive numbers.

6-Digit Scramble 1

Place the numbers 1 through 6 in the blanks to form a six-digit number.
It's not easy! You have to follow all of these rules:

↳ The first two digits (starting on the left) must
   be divisible by 2.

↳ The first three digits must be divisible by 3.

↳ The first four digits must be divisible by 4.

↳ The first five digits must be divisible by 5.

↳ The six-digit number must be divisible by 6.

THINK ABOUT IT!

↳ Use divisibility rules to narrow down the
   choices for each place. For instance, numbers divisible by 5 must end in what number?

↳ Are numbers divisible by 2 even or odd?

↳ Are numbers divisible by 4 even or odd?

↳ Numbers divisible by 6 are also divisible by which two numbers?

____ ____ ____ , ____ ____ ____

_____ ÷ 2 = _____

_____ ÷ 3 = _____

_____ ÷ 4 = _____

_____ ÷ 5 = _____

_____ ÷ 6 = _____

BIG FAT HINT The digits form a pattern when correctly placed.
• Make a table to help you identify possible choices for each place.
• Use a calculator to check your work.

Name _____ Date _____

6-Digit Scramble 2

Place the numbers 4 through 9 in the blanks to form a six-digit number.
Follow all of these rules:

↳ The first two digits (starting on the left) must be divisible by 2.

↳ The first three digits must be divisible by 3.

↳ The first four digits must be divisible by 4.

↳ The first five digits must be divisible by 5.

↳ The six-digit number must be divisible by 6.

_____ _____ _____ , _____ _____ _____

_____ ÷ 2 = _____

_____ ÷ 3 = _____

_____ ÷ 4 = _____

_____ ÷ 5 = _____

_____ ÷ 6 = _____

THINK ABOUT IT!

Use divisibility rules to narrow down the choices for each place.
For instance, numbers divisible by 5 must end in what number?

BIG FAT HINT Use a calculator to check your work.

Name _____ Date _____

7-Digit Scramble

Place the numbers 2 through 8 in the blanks
to form a seven-digit number. Follow these rules:

↳ The first two digits (starting on the left) must be divisible by 2.

↳ The first three digits must be divisible by 3.

↳ The first four digits must be divisible by 4

↳ The first five digits must be divisible by 5.

↳ The first six digits must be divisible by 6.

↳ The entire number must be divisible by 7.

_____ , _____ _____ _____ , _____ _____ _____

_____ ÷ 2 = _____

_____ ÷ 3 = _____

_____ ÷ 4 = _____

_____ ÷ 5 = _____

_____ ÷ 6 = _____

_____ ÷ 7 = _____

THINK ABOUT IT!

Use divisibility rules to narrow down the choices for each place.
For instance, the first two-digit number is divisible by 2 and so must be even.

38 Numbers and Arithmetic

BIG FAT HINT Use a calculator to check your work.

101 Brain-Boosting Math Puzzles Scholastic Professional Books

Dates and Places

Can you fit each of these dates and numbers in this puzzle? You can use a date or number only one time. Cross off each date and number as you use it.

3-Digit Numbers
101
~~201~~
409
417
601
602
902
999
Dates
1588
1776
1812
1849
1914
1929
1969
1976
1984
2044
5-Digit Numbers
12,185
45,678
75,121
77,964

2 0 1

THINK ABOUT IT!

↳ Study the numbers in the dates column. What digits do they have in common?

↳ Which digits are unique (one of a kind)? Fill in the numbers with unique digits first.

101 Brain-Boosting Math Puzzles   Scholastic Professional Books

Name _____ Date _____

Number Circle 1

Does the number 7 ring a bell? Think about it: the 7 dwarfs, 7 days a week, the movie and TV show *The Magnificent Seven*, lucky 7, 7 wonders of the world, and so on. What other noteworthy numbers do you know? Solve the clues and fill the puzzle with familiar numbers.

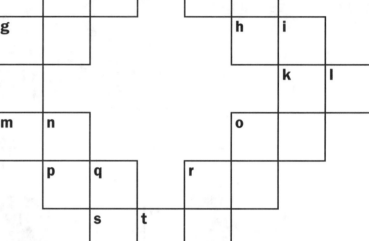

Across

a. _____ *Dalmatians*

d. number of cards in a standard deck

e. _____ *Tears* (1960s song)

g. number of days in September

h. an unlucky number

j. patriotic-sounding gas station

k. historic highway route

m. usual age of retirement

o. number of seconds in a minute

p. Century _____ (a real estate company)

r. sweet _____

s. number of days in a year

Down

a. number of zodiac signs

b. nought

c. the digits add up to 10.

d. number of U.S. states

f. the Roman numeral LXI

g. number of days in a leap year

i. number of degrees in a circle

j. number of continents

l. half a dozen

n. _____ Pick-Up (a game)

o. a number divisible by 2, 3, 6, and 11

q. a baker's dozen

r. the Ides of March

t. number of feet in 2 yards

THINK ABOUT IT!

Which clues can you look up in reference sources?

101 Brain-Boosting Math Puzzles Scholastic Professional Books

BIG FAT HINT o. DOWN and k. ACROSS are both 66.

Name _____ Date _____

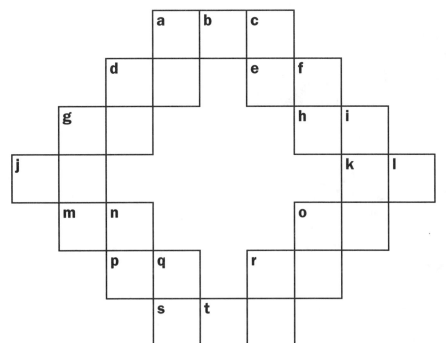

Solve the clues and fill the puzzle with familiar numbers.

Across

a. telephone number to dial in an emergency

d. statehood rank of Alaska

e. number of hours in a day

g. eight touchdowns with one extra point missed

h. the Roman numeral LXXXII

j. _____ winks (a short nap)

k. popular teen magazine

m. number of days in week minus 3

o. the Roman numeral LII

p. the legal voting age

r. three score, plus 10 (Hint: One score equals 20.)

s. Secret agent James Bond is _____.

Down

a. a number divisible by 3, 9, and 11

b. value of a foul shot in basketball

c. a dozen

d. the last year of World War II: 19_____

f. number of states in the continental United States

g. half of a millennium

i. the boiling point of water (Fahrenheit degrees)

j. number of seasons

l. a lucky number

n. two score, plus 1

o. half a century

q. four score

r. the digits add up to 14

t. "love" in tennis

THINK ABOUT IT!

↳ Which answers can you look up in reference books?

↳ Missing one digit of a number? Plug in all the possible digits to see which digit fits in the puzzle best.

101 Brain-Boosting Math Puzzles Scholastic Professional Books

BIG FAT HINT James Bond is agent 007 (s Across).
The boiling point of water is 212°F (i Down).

Gearing Up

Each gear has 12 cogs (bits that mesh with other bits).
If Gear A makes one complete revolution (turn), so will Gear B.

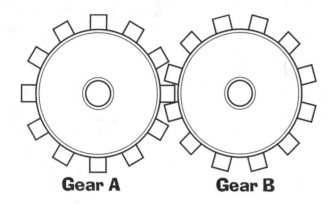

Gear A   **Gear B**

For each of the examples below, if Gear A makes one revolution, how many revolutions will Gear B make?

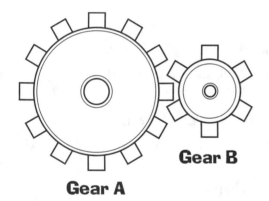

Gear B

Gear A

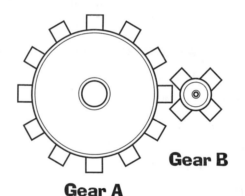

Gear B

Gear A

1. _____

2. _____

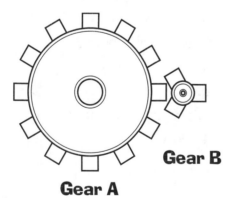

Gear B

Gear A

3. _____

THINK ABOUT IT!

Count the cogs on both gears. What is the ratio of cogs on Gear A to cogs on Gear B?

BIG FAT HINT Divide the cogs on Gear A by the cogs on Gear B.

101 Brain-Boosting Math Puzzles   Scholastic Professional Books

E.S.P. Number

You can use this Extra-Sure Problem to read someone's mind with no problem. It's okay to use a calculator with this problem. Here's how it works:

1. Someone, somewhere, is thinking of a number between 6,100 and 6,200. To read this person's mind, think of any four numbers from 1 through 9.

_____

2. Write these four numbers as the greatest 4-digit number possible.

_____

3. Write the four numbers as the least 4-digit number possible.

_____

4. Subtract the lesser number from the greater number.

Greater Number:

Lesser Number: − _____

Difference:

5. Is the difference a number between 6,100 and 6,200? If it is—eureka! You found the number. If your difference is *not* between 6,100 and 6,200, go on to the next step.

6. Circle the difference in Step 4. Using this number, go back to Step 2.

Keep repeating the steps until you get a number from 6,100 to 6,200.

THINK ABOUT IT!

Try this trick with four new numbers. How long does it take to get the magic answer? Be patient!

101 Brain-Boosting Math Puzzles   Scholastic Professional Books

BIG FAT HINT No matter which four numbers you pick, you will always end up with the same 4-digit number.

Pot of Gold 1

Which of the four pots is the *real* pot of gold? To find out, start at the leprechaun. Then move north, south, east, or west according to the directions. The first pot of gold that you land on is the real one.

Example: The first move is 1 East. That means you move one square to the right of the leprechaun.

Move in these directions to find the pot of gold:

1 East

1 South

3 West

5 North

1 East

2 South

2 East

1 South

2 West

2 North

3 West

1 North

5 East

THINK ABOUT IT!

If a move takes you off the grid, you made a mistake. Start over.

BIG FAT HINT You may reach the pot of gold before finishing the list of moves.

101 Brain-Boosting Math Puzzles   Scholastic Professional Books

Name _____ Date _____

Pot of Gold 2

Which of the four pots really contains gold? To find out, start at the leprechaun. Then move north, south, east, west, northeast, southeast, northwest, or southwest according to the directions. You may pass through a square that contains a pot during a move. The first pot that you *land on* contains gold.

Example: The first move is **1 Southeast**. Move one square diagonally to the bottom right square of the grid.

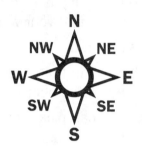

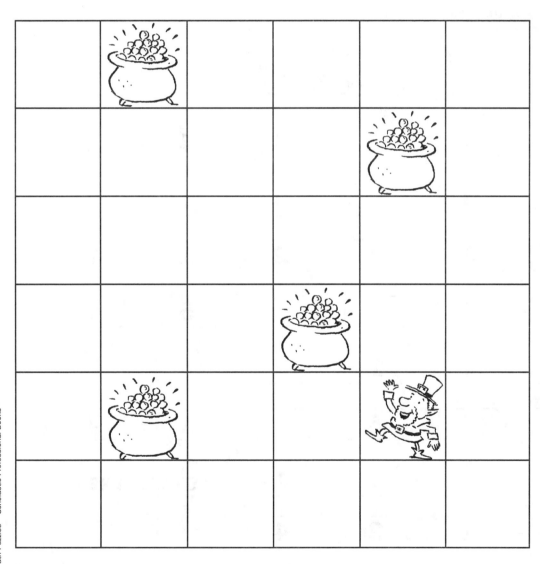

Move in these directions to find the pot of gold:

1 Southeast

5 North

3 Southwest

2 West

2 Northeast

2 Southeast

3 West

2 North

1 East

1 Northwest

3 South

2 East

2 North

1 East

THINK ABOUT IT!

If a move takes you off the grid, you made a mistake. Start over.

BIG FAT HINT You may reach the pot of gold before finishing the list of moves.

Geometry and Coordinates 45

101 Brain-Boosting Math Puzzles   Scholastic Professional Books

Escape from Antcatraz

You're a tiny ant, trapped underground on the number 2 indicated.
Can you find your way and crawl back to the surface? Here's how:

↳ Pick a direction—north, south, east, or west.

↳ Move in that direction. You can move only the number of spaces indicated
   by the number you're on. (Your first move is 2 spaces, for example.)

↳ You can pick a new direction at the beginning of a move
   but you cannot change direction in the middle of a move.

↳ If you wander off the anthill, you're doomed.

THINK ABOUT IT!

What is the last number on the grid that you will hit? What is the second number?

BIG FAT HINT The shortest path is 7 moves long. If
you're still crawling around after 7 moves, stop and start over.

101 Brain-Boosting Math Puzzles Scholastic Professional Books

Gem Tones 1

Can you color this gemstone using only four colors? What's the hitch? No two neighboring spaces (spaces that share a side) can be the same color.

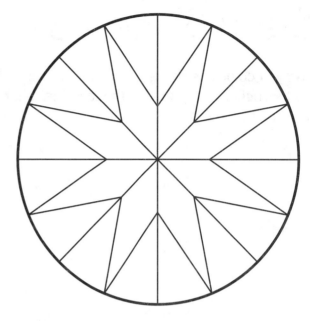

THINK ABOUT IT!

Plot your moves with a pencil first. For example, assign a letter to each color—a, b, c, and d. Then write the letters in the gem before you color the spaces.

BIG FAT HINT The gem is symmetrical. You can divide it in half to make identical sides. Once you color one half of the gem, the other half should be easy!

Gem Tones 2

Can you color this gemstone using only four colors? What's the hitch? No two neighboring spaces (spaces that share a side) can be the same color.

THINK ABOUT IT!

Plot your moves with a pencil first. For example, assign a letter to each color—a, b, c, and d. Then write the letters in the gem before you color the spaces.

BIG FAT HINT The gem is symmetrical. You can divide it in half to make identical sides. Once you color one half of the gem, the other half should be easy!

101 Brain-Boosting Math Puzzles Scholastic Professional Books

Gem Tones 3

Can you color this gemstone using only four colors?
No two neighboring spaces (spaces that share a
side) can be the same color.

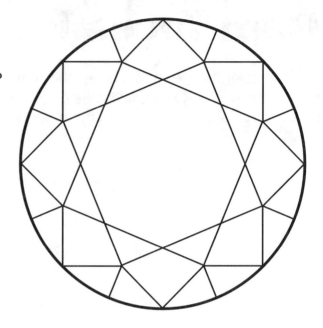

THINK ABOUT IT!

Plot your moves with a pencil first. For example, assign a
letter to each color—a, b, c, and d. Then write the letters
in the gem before you color the spaces.

BIG FAT HINT The gem is symmetrical. You
can divide it in half to make identical sides. Once you
color one half of the gem, the other half should be easy!

3-D Cube

Can you draw a cube? Remember—a cube
has six identical squares for sides. Here's
a shortcut: Start with the two-dimensional
hexagon shown. Then draw three lines to
turn it into a three-dimensional cube.

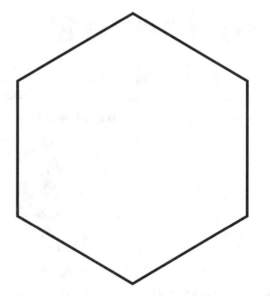

THINK ABOUT IT!

How many ways could the cube be facing? For example, is it sitting on a side or a point?

BIG FAT HINT All three lines that you draw
should be contained within the hexagon.

Dream House

Can you trace this dream house without lifting your pencil? Start at any point. You can pass through a point more than once but you *cannot* draw the same line twice.

THINK ABOUT IT!

- What is the best starting point? Why?
- Count the exits and entrances at each point. What do you notice?

BIG FAT HINT Start at one of the two points that have an odd number of exits and entrances (3). You'll end up at a different point.

Letter Letter

Mirror, mirror, on the wall—
Which letters are most symmetrical?

Symmetry means dividing an image in half to form two mirror images. The letters E, M, and V are symmetrical. The letter F is not symmetrical.

Here are all 26 letters in capitals.

**A B C D E F G H I J K L M
N O P Q R S T U V W X Y Z**

Some letters have double symmetry. You can divide them in half two ways. The letter H has double symmetry.

Including the letter H, there are four letters that have double symmetry. What are the other three letters?

THINK ABOUT IT!

Cut a letter in half with a vertical line and a horizontal line.
Then try drawing diagonal lines that pass through the middle of the letter.

BIG FAT HINT One of the letters with double symmetry is I. Do you see why?

101 Brain-Boosting Math Puzzles Scholastic Professional Books

Six Ugly Bugs

These six bugs are so ugly that they can't stand the sight of each other!
Can you place all six in the garden so that no bug is in line with another?
This means that the bugs can't be in the same row, column, or diagonal.

Cut out the bugs and place them on the grid.

THINK ABOUT IT!

↪ Guess and check is one strategy to use to solve this problem.

↪ Another strategy is to place all the bugs in different rows.
    Then move them up and down in the columns until none of the bugs line up.

101 Brain-Boosting Math Puzzles   Scholastic Professional Books

BIG FAT HINT Don't put a bug in any of the four corners.

Name _____ Date _____

Creepy Crawly Corral

Four ants, four bees, four cockroaches, and four dragonflies live on Creepy Crawly Ranch. The rancher hates to put two of any kind of insect in one corral. If she did, she'd be overrun with too many of one kind of insect. Draw fences to create four corrals that each contain four different insects. Each side of the fence must be either vertical (up and down) or horizontal (side to side). No diagonals are allowed.

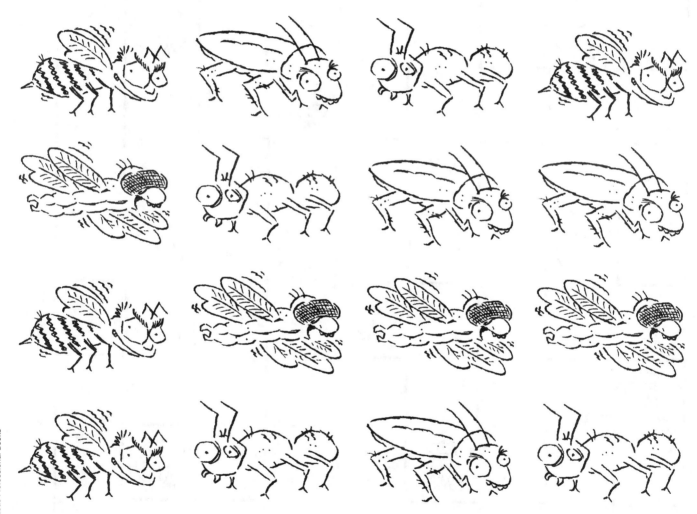

THINK ABOUT IT!

↳ How will the four corrals compare to each other in size?

↳ How many shapes can the corrals be? For example, one possible shape is an L-shape.

BIG FAT HINT The four insects in the last column all belong in the same corral.

Geometry and Coordinates 51

101 Brain-Boosting Math Puzzles Scholastic Professional Books

Sheepish Grid

Nine sheep live at the Sheepish Grid Ranch. Not all the sheep live inside the corral. How many sheep are inside the corral and how many are outside?

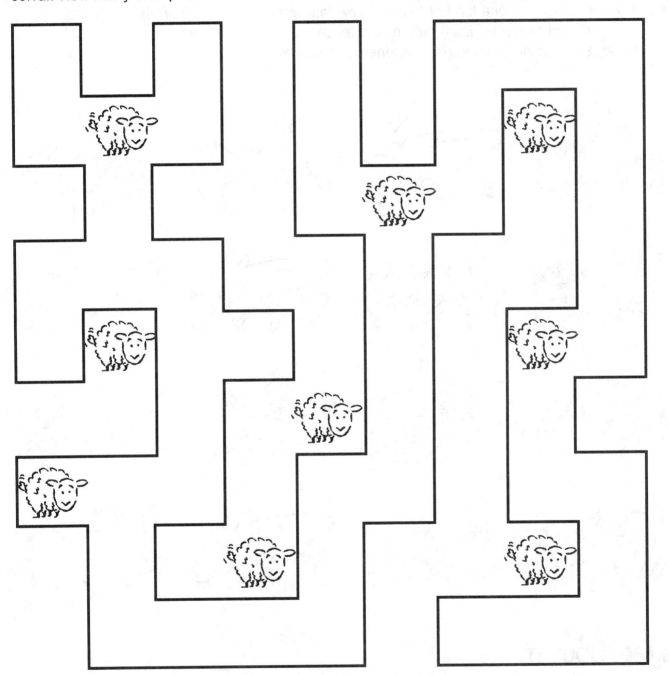

THINK ABOUT IT!

Pick a sheep. Can you lead it outside the corral without going through a fence?

BIG FAT HINT Pick an area of the corral and shade it with your pencil. Is the area completely enclosed, or does your shading spill outside?

101 Brain-Boosting Math Puzzles   Scholastic Professional Books

Name _____ Date _____

Fats Domino

Look at the pattern of dots inside the man.
Cut out and then arrange all 12 dominos
to create exactly the same pattern.

THINK ABOUT IT!

Which domino has a twin?

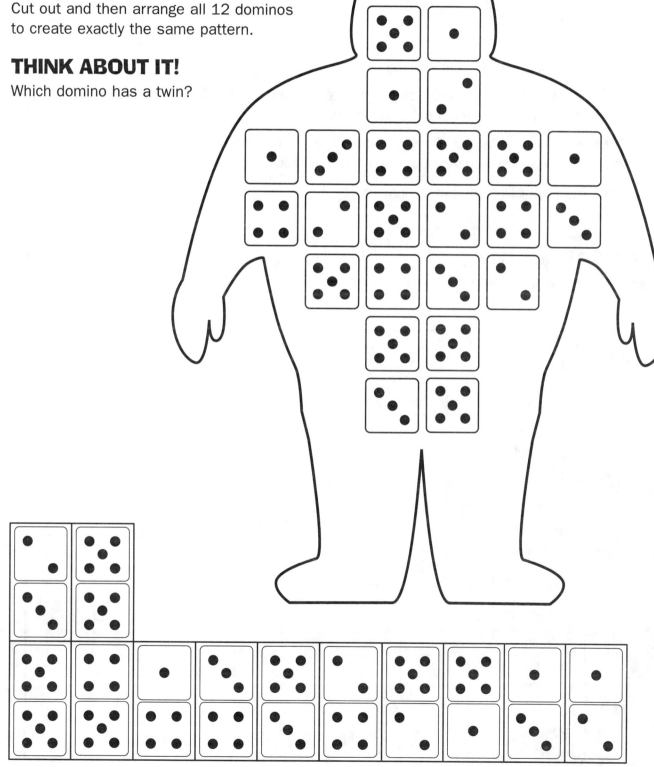

BIG FAT HINT Look at the dominoes that have 3 dots on one half of them.
Which way do the dots slant? Use this slant to help you position these dominoes.

101 Brain-Boosting Math Puzzles   Scholastic Professional Books

Paper Door

Can you walk through a hole in this piece of paper?
Before you say, "No way!," try this:

1. Cut out this rectangle.

2. Fold in half along the thin solid line.

3. Cut along the dotted lines. Be careful not to cut beyond the dotted lines!
   Notice that they stop just short of the edge.

4. Cut the solid line. Careful! Don't cut the paper all the way in half.
   You should have two connected strips on either side.

5. Open the Paper Door and walk right through!

THINK ABOUT IT!

Can you fit through a hole in a 5 × 7 index card?

101 Brain-Boosting Math Puzzles   Scholastic Professional Books

BIG FAT HINT Follow the same pattern of cuts as
on the paper door. Make the strips as narrow as you can.

Smell the Roses

Cut out the shape along the outside border. Fold it in half so that all the images are facing out. Paste or glue together the blank sides. Make two folds as shown to form a square.

Can you refold the square so that one side comes up all roses? How many other square patterns can you make?

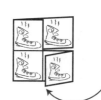

THINK ABOUT IT!

Substitute your own pictures or messages to make an original square puzzle!

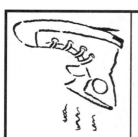  

BIG FAT HINT
• Four roses on the front means that there will be four smelly sneakers on the back.
• Form squares only. Do not form cubes.

Geometry and Coordinates 55

Boxed In

Each of these eight boxes is a cube—a figure with six equal, square sides. Each outside square has the name of a product stamped on it. Study the picture and answer the questions.

1. How many squares are there in all? _____

2. How many squares are stamped? _____

3. How many squares are *not* stamped? _____

THINK ABOUT IT!

Make a model using building blocks or other cubes.

BIG FAT HINT The four squares on the bottom are outside, so they are stamped.

101 Brain-Boosting Math Puzzles   Scholastic Professional Books

5 to 1

Can you turn these 5 squares into 1 big square?

↳ Cut out the 5-square shape.

↳ Then cut it into pieces along the dashed lines.

↳ Arrange the pieces into 1 square.

THINK ABOUT IT!

How will the area of the large square compare
to the area of the five smaller squares?

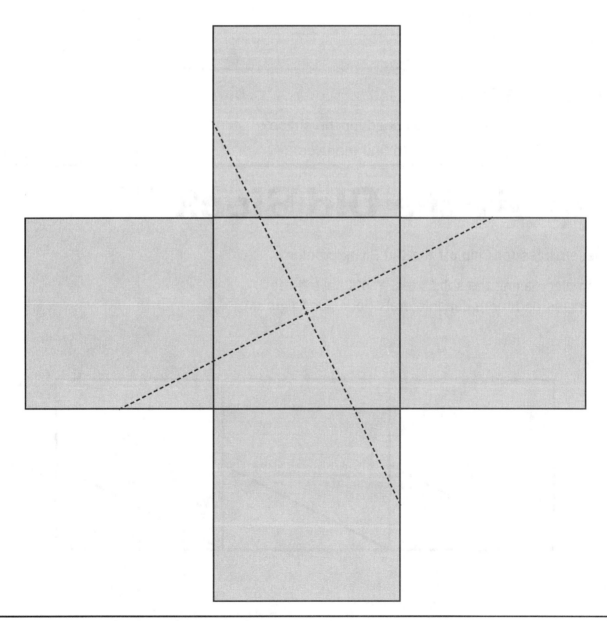

101 Brain-Boosting Math Puzzles Scholastic Professional Books

BIG FAT HINT You can rotate (turn), translate
(slide), and overlap the pieces, but you can't flip them.

Geometry and Coordinates 57

Chip off the Old Block 1

Can you form this shape with
the Chip off the Old Block
pieces shown below?

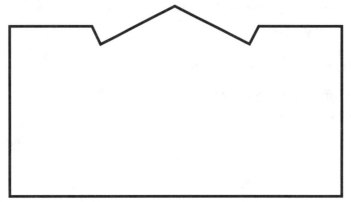

THINK ABOUT IT!

↪ How many of the pieces do you need for the shape?

↪ Draw lines through the shapes to find triangles.

BIG FAT HINT You can rotate (turn),
reflect (flip), or translate (slide) the pieces.

Chip off the Old Block

Use these pieces for Chip off the Old Block problems.

Cut each piece along the solid lines. You'll have three
right triangles and three quadrilaterals (four-sided figures).

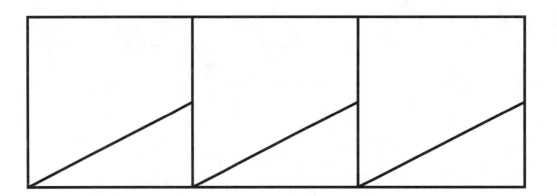

101 Brain-Boosting Math Puzzles   Scholastic Professional Books

Name _____   Date _____

Chip off the Old Block 2

Can you form this shape with the Chip off the Old Block pieces?

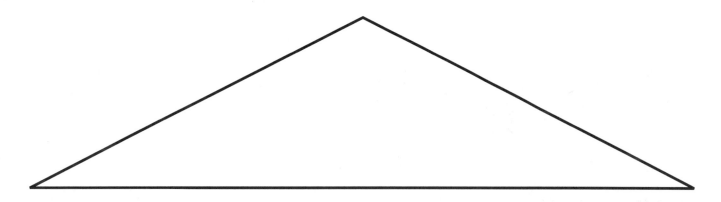

THINK ABOUT IT!

↳ How many of the pieces do you need for the shape?

↳ Draw lines through the shapes to find triangles.

BIG FAT HINT You can rotate (turn), reflect (flip), or translate (slide) the pieces.

Name _____   Date _____

Chip off the Old Block 3

Can you form this shape with the Chip off the Old Block pieces?

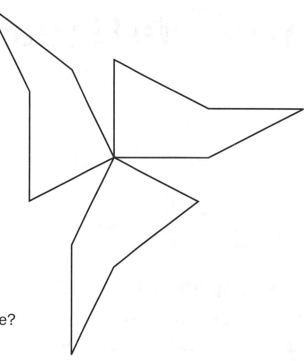

What other shapes can you make?

THINK ABOUT IT!

↳ How many of the pieces do you need for the shape?

↳ Draw lines through the shapes to find triangles.

BIG FAT HINT Rotate (turn), reflect (flip), or translate (slide) the pieces.

101 Brain-Boosting Math Puzzles   Scholastic Professional Books

Triangle Triangle

Cut out the seven triangles. Then rotate (turn) and translate (slide) them to form one large equilateral triangle. Remember—an equilateral triangle has three equal sides and three equal angles.

THINK ABOUT IT!

↳ Which triangles have sides of the same length?

↳ Which triangles are right triangles (have a 90° angle)?

↳ Which triangles are identical?

BIG FAT HINT Put the largest triangle at the top. Use four triangles to form a square right below it.

Triangle Square

Using the seven triangles from Triangle Triangle, form a perfect square.

THINK ABOUT IT!

↳ A square has four corners. Each corner measures 90°.

↳ Which triangles have angles of 90°?

BIG FAT HINT Opposite corners have identical triangles.

101 Brain-Boosting Math Puzzles Scholastic Professional Books

Name _____   Date _____

Triangle Circle

These two circles are identical. Can you use them to draw a perfect equilateral triangle? Can you use them to draw two equilateral triangles, with one triangle twice as tall as the other? You may use a ruler to draw the lines.

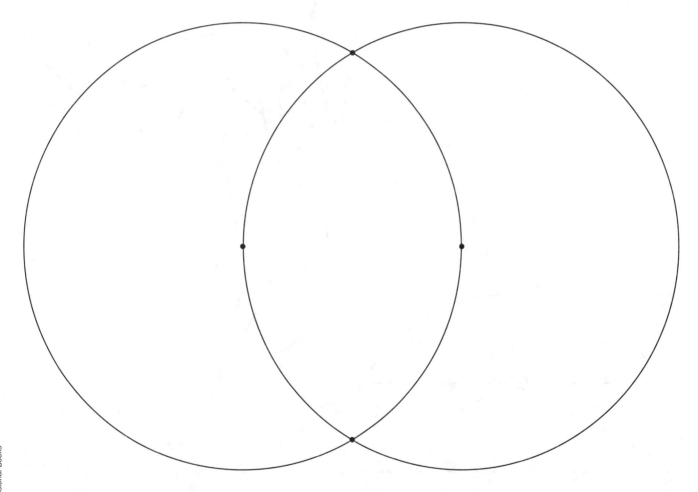

THINK ABOUT IT!

↳ A straight line is the shortest distance between two points.
   How does this fact help you draw a bigger triangle?

BIG FAT HINT Connect the centers of the
two circles to form the base of the triangle.

Geometry and Coordinates | 61

101 Brain-Boosting Math Puzzles   Scholastic Professional Books

Circle 10

Can you make this shape using the
pieces below? Cut out the pieces
along the dashed lines. What other
shapes can you make?

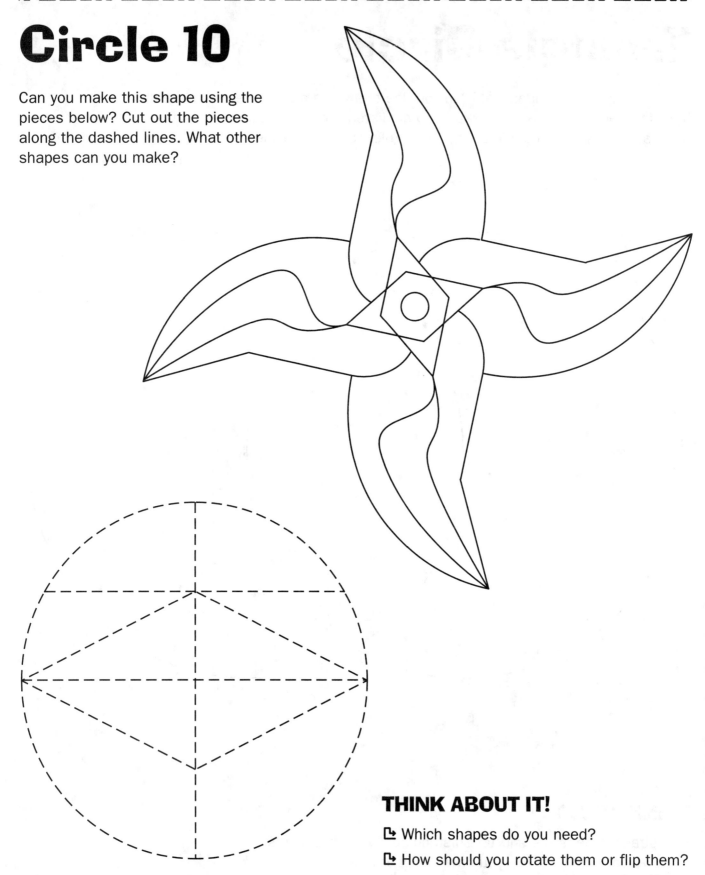

THINK ABOUT IT!

↳ Which shapes do you need?

↳ How should you rotate them or flip them?

BIG FAT HINT Trace the outline of the shape onto
paper. Without the decorations, the problem is easier to solve.

101 Brain-Boosting Math Puzzles   Scholastic Professional Books

Name _____ Date _____

Shell-Shocked

How many whole sand dollar shells are there?

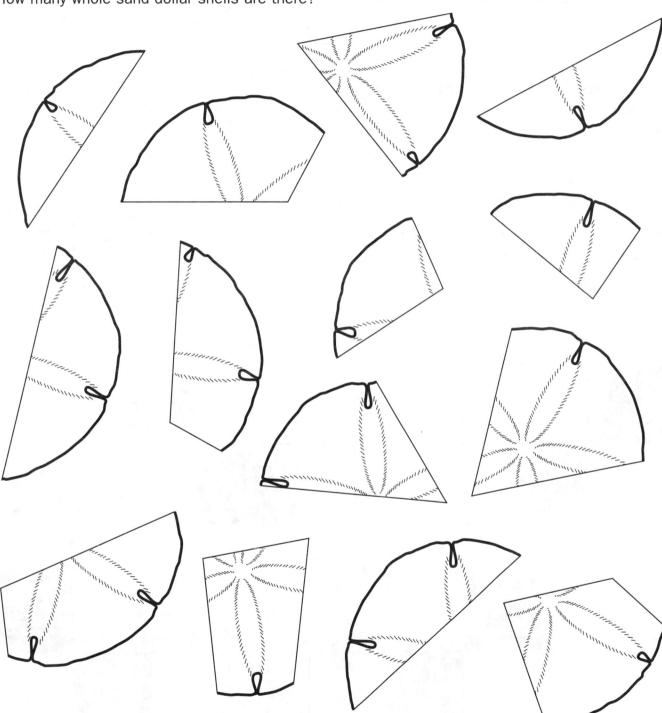

THINK ABOUT IT!

How many "notches" and "petals" does each sand dollar have?

BIG FAT HINT Stuck? Cut out the pieces
and fit them together like a jigsaw puzzle.

Geometry and Coordinates 63

101 Brain-Boosting Math Puzzles   Scholastic Professional Books

Checkered Past 1

Can you form a checkerboard with these 4 tile pieces? Cut out the pieces. Then arrange them according to these rules:

↳ None of the pieces can overlap.

↳ Each side of the checkerboard must have 4 squares.

↳ The squares must alternate between black and white.

THINK ABOUT IT!

↳ If you get stuck, rotate (turn) or replace the tiles.

↳ You *cannot* flip the tiles over.

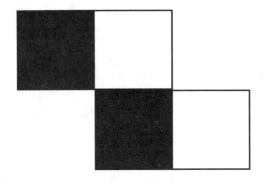

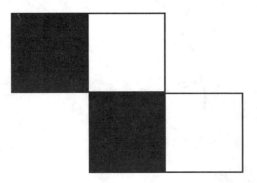

BIG FAT HINT • The upper left hand and lower right hand corners are white.
• Place an L-shaped piece in both of these corners.

101 Brain-Boosting Math Puzzles   Scholastic Professional Books

Checkered Past 2

Can you form a checkerboard with these 9 tile pieces? Cut out the pieces. Then arrange them according to the following rules:

↳ None of the pieces can overlap.

↳ Each side of the checkerboard must have 6 squares.

↳ The squares must alternate between black and white.

THINK ABOUT IT!

↳ If you get stuck, rotate (turn) or replace the tiles.

↳ You *cannot* flip the tiles over.

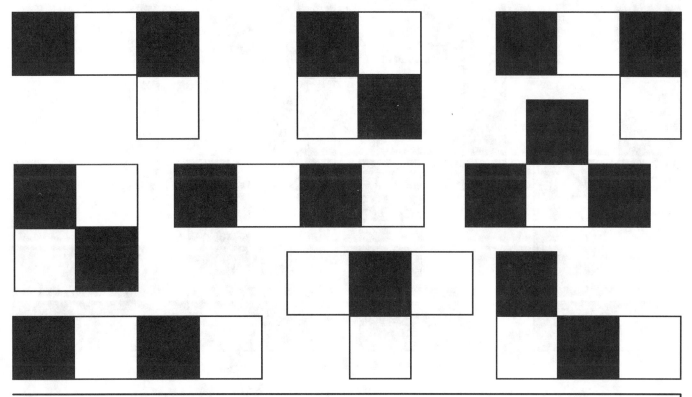

101 Brain-Boosting Math Puzzles   Scholastic Professional Books

BIG FAT HINT • The upper left hand and lower right hand corners are white. • Place an L-shaped piece in one of these corners.

Geometry and Coordinates | 65 |

Name _____   Date _____

Even Stevens

The Stevens octuplets (eight babies born at the same time) inherit an equal share of the family farm. Each share is the same size and shape—a four-square L-shaped plot of land. But the shape might be rotated. Can you divide the farm into eight equal shares, each one with a Stevens octuplet on it? (The Stevens octuplet might be on any one of his or her four squares.)

THINK ABOUT IT!

Which L-shaped plots can you put down right away?

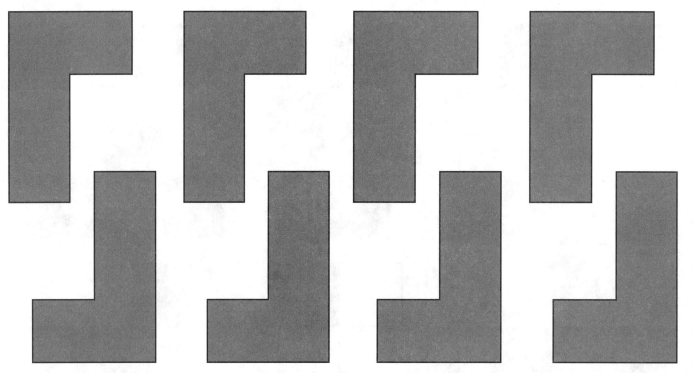

BIG FAT HINT Only two of the four-square plots border the farmhouse.

101 Brain-Boosting Math Puzzles   Scholastic Professional Books

Balanced Valance

Each of the Valance septuplets (seven babies born at the same time) owns an equal plot of five acres (one acre per square). Can you balance the Valance plots on this six-acre by six-acre parcel of land? The plots may be rotated (turned) or reflected (flipped). Each plot must have one Valance sister on it.

THINK ABOUT IT!

↳ Which plots can you put down right away?

↳ How many plots can border one side?

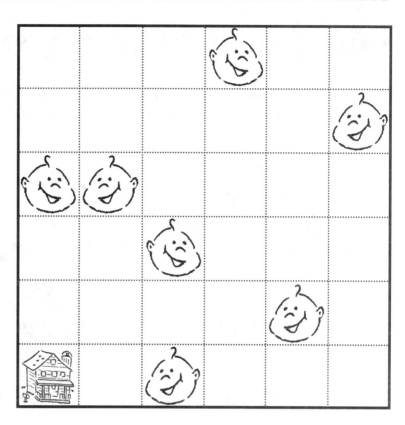

BIG FAT HINT Only two plots border the house.

Geometry and Coordinates 67

Name _____   Date _____

Mirror Match-Up

Can you arrange these 9 cards into a 3-by-3 square? There's a catch!
Each shape must be next to its mirror image—the flipped version of itself.

THINK ABOUT IT!

↳ What four mirror images are possible?

↳ Which two designs look the same when flipped?

101 Brain-Boosting Math Puzzles   Scholastic Professional Books

BIG FAT HINT In the bottom two rows, the posies and the four-pointed stars are in exactly the same positions.

Victor's Vector

The direction of an airplane is called a *vector*. Easterly Airline is moving east at 400 miles per hour. Northern Skyway is heading north at 600 miles per hour. Wild West Jets is heading west at 500 miles per hour. All three planes are at the same altitude (height). Victor, an air traffic controller, is almost certain that two planes will crash if they continue on their present course.

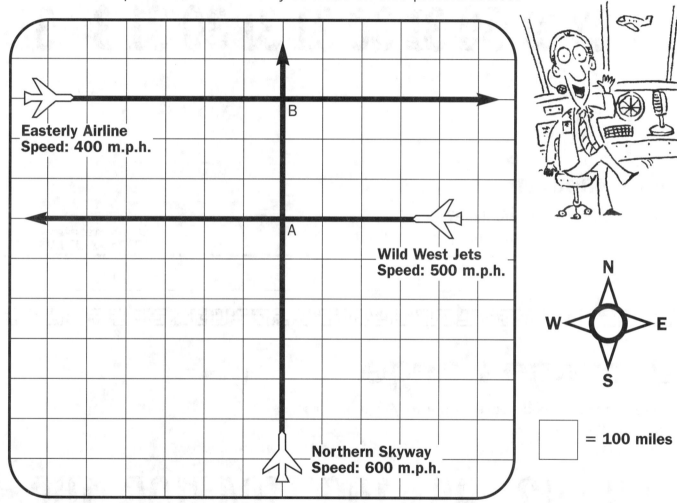

Easterly Airline Speed: 400 m.p.h.

B

A

Wild West Jets Speed: 500 m.p.h.

Northern Skyway Speed: 600 m.p.h.

N
W   E
S

☐ = 100 miles

1. Which planes will crash? _____

2. At which point (A or B) will they crash? _____

3. In how many hours and minutes will they crash? _____

THINK ABOUT IT!

Where will each plane be in exactly one hour?

BIG FAT HINT Wild West and Easterly will cross the same point (A), but not at the same time.

101 Brain-Boosting Math Puzzles   Scholastic Professional Books

31 Up

Where would you find these numbers in this order?

31 28 31 30 31 30 31 31 30 31 30 31

THINK ABOUT IT!

⤷ How many numbers are there?

⤷ What is odd about the pattern?

BIG FAT HINT Every four years, the number 28 becomes 29.

Strange Range

These numbers appear together in a very common place.
Where do they appear?

88   92   96   100   104 106 108

THINK ABOUT IT!

⤷ What is the range of numbers?

⤷ What could numbers in this range stand for?

⤷ Do you see a pattern?

BIG FAT HINT You often find the following set of numbers in the same place: 530, 600, 700, 800, 1000, 1200, 1400, 1700.

101 Brain-Boosting Math Puzzles   Scholastic Professional Books

Name _____ Date _____

Area Code Explosion

Many cities and towns are getting new telephone area codes.
The old area codes follow a pattern. Many new area codes
break this pattern. What's the pattern? What do the old area
codes have in common that these new area codes don't?

Old Area Codes			
202	212	213	303
313	312	616	904

New Area Codes			
248	330	352	562
573	734	847	888

THINK ABOUT IT!

What is your area code? Is it an old one or a new one?

BIG FAT HINT Look at the middle digits.

Name _____ Date _____

Zip Code Geography

Look at the five zip codes
for the states shown at
right. What conclusion can
you draw about zip codes
and the geographic
locations of these states?

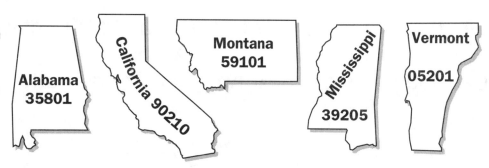

Alabama 35801

California 90210

Montana 59101

Mississippi 39205

Vermont 05201

THINK ABOUT IT!

↳ Order the states in terms of their geography—north/south or east/west.
  (Use a map if you like.)

↳ Order the zip codes from least to greatest.

BIG FAT HINT Place the states in order from east to west.

Logical Thinking 71

101 Brain-Boosting Math Puzzles   Scholastic Professional Books

Secrets of the Interstates—Unlocked!

Interstate highways run through several states. Each number is a code for its geography— where the interstate is on a national map. Look at the list in the box. Can you unlock the secret interstate code?

Interstate	Direction	Sample Cities Connected
5	North-South	Portland, OR, and Los Angeles, CA
20	East-West	Dallas, TX, and Jackson, MS
25	North-South	Denver, CO, and Albuquerque, NM
35	North-South	Des Moines, IA, and Kansas City, MO
40	East-West	Albuquerque, NM, and Oklahoma City, OK
55	North-South	Memphis, TN, and Jackson, MS
65	North-South	Louisville, KY, and Nashville, TN
70	East-West	Denver, CO, and Kansas City, MO
90	East-West	Sioux Falls, SD, and Boise, ID
95	North-South	Richmond, VA, and Miami, FL

THINK ABOUT IT!

⤷ What do the numbers of the east-west interstates have in common?
the north-south interstates?

⤷ A north-south interstate connects Atlanta, Georgia, and Cincinnati, Ohio.
Both cities are just east of Nashville. Based on the table,
can you give the interstate's number?

BIG FAT HINT Arrange the cities on east-west interstates from south to north. (Use a map if you like.) Notice any patterns?

Year to Year

What do the years 1771, 1881, and 1991 have in common?

Can you name the next two years in the pattern?

_____ and _____

THINK ABOUT IT!

⤷ In what centuries are the three numbers?
⤷ In what century will the next date be?

BIG FAT HINT The three examples come at the end of a century; the next year comes at the beginning of a century.

101 Brain-Boosting Math Puzzles   Scholastic Professional Books

Time Line

Picture the times below on an analog clock
(one with an hour and a minute hand).
What pattern do they have in common?

1:05

3:16

5:27

7:33

9:50

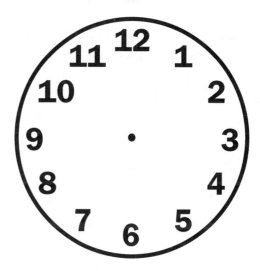

THINK ABOUT IT!

Draw pictures of the times on the clock to make the pattern clearer.

BIG FAT HINT
12:00 also fits the pattern.

Search in Vain

A vanity license plate spells out a phrase using
numbers and letters.

Example: W84U stands for "Wait (w + eight) for you."

Search the rows, columns, and diagonals in the
puzzle to find all the regular license plate numbers.
listed in the box The leftover letters and numbers,
when unscrambled, spell out a vanity plate greeting.

```
G B 7 4 0 G
5 T G 2 1 5
4 8 4 2 U 4
1 R 5 1 C 3
X T 2 4 5 C
B G 7 2 1 R
```

List of License Plates
BX145G
XT245C
BG721R
GB740G
BT521G
GT415R
RC345G

THINK ABOUT IT!

⤷ Study the list of numbers and letters and find a pattern.

⤷ In which places are there numbers and in which places are there letters
in each plate? How can this fact help you find the plate numbers faster?

BIG FAT HINT There are six leftover
numbers and letters. The G and R come first.

101 Brain-Boosting Math Puzzles Scholastic Professional Books

Name _____ Date _____

Victor's Victory 1

Victor, an air traffic controller, aced the air traffic control test.
For part of the test, he had to pick out patterns of symbols.
Can you match Victor's perfect score? For each set of symbols,
circle the one (a, b, or c) that best completes the pattern.
State in words why your answer fits the pattern.

1.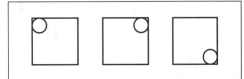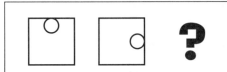

a. **b.** **c.**

2.

a. **b.** **c.**

3.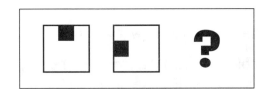

a. **b.** **c.**

THINK ABOUT IT!

The first three symbols belong in a set. The second three symbols
belong in a different, but similar, set. Describe each set in words.

101 Brain-Boosting Math Puzzles Scholastic Professional Books

BIG FAT HINT The rule for the first problem
is to rotate the shape 90 degrees clockwise each time.

Victor's Victory 2

Victor, an air traffic controller, aced his second air traffic control test. Can you match his perfect score? For each set of symbols, circle the one (a, b, or c) that best completes the pattern.

1.

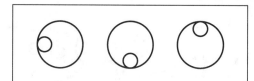 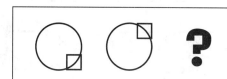

    a.   **b.**   **c.**

2.

    a.   **b.**   **c.**

3.

    a.   **b.**   **c.**

THINK ABOUT IT!

↳ The first three symbols belong in a set.

↳ The second three symbols belong in a different, but similar, set.

↳ After you choose an answer, can you state in a sentence why it fits the pattern?

BIG FAT HINT The rule for the first problem is to rotate the shape 90 degrees to the left and then 180 degrees right or left.

Klepto Cat

Klepto Cat can't stop stealing. To catch this feline thief, read the statements from the witness to one of Klepto's burglaries. Narrow down the suspects to one guilty cat who fits all the facts.

Witness Statements

1. The cat didn't have stripes.
2. The cat had a tail.
3. The cat had pointy ears and a collar.
4. The theif's name did not start with the letter *S*.

THINK ABOUT IT!

Which clues eliminate (rule out) the most cats? Start with those clues. Then move on to the other ones.

BIG FAT HINT The guilty cat has no stripes, a tail, pointy ears, a collar, and a name that starts with the letter *P*.

Klepto Cat Returns

Klepto Cat likes to steal clothes. But this feline thief doesn't take just any clothes. Look at the pictures of the stolen items. Use logic to figure out what all the items of clothing have in common.

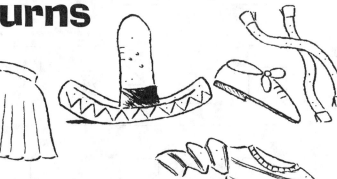

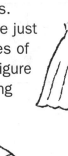

THINK ABOUT IT!

What are the attributes (traits) of the clothes? What are the names of the clothes? Make a list.

BIG FAT HINT Klepto Cat never steals dresses, blouses, handkerchiefs, underwear, or pajamas.

101 Brain-Boosting Math Puzzles Scholastic Professional Books

Son of Klepto Cat

Klepto Cat may be a feline thief. But his son is definitely not. In fact, Klepto Cat's son shares only one trait with his father. Look at Klepto Cat. Then look at the five kittens. Which one is Klepto Cat's son?

THINK ABOUT IT!

↳ Make a list of Klepto Cat's attributes (traits).

↳ Which kitties can you eliminate (rule out)?

BIG FAT HINT Klepto Cat's attributes include no stripes, a tail, pointy ears, and a collar.

Triple Play 1

Quick! What is 33,333 × 33,333? Hint: You don't need a calculator to figure it out. Study this number pattern to come up with the answer.

$$3 \times 3 = 9$$

$$33 \times 33 = 1,089$$

$$333 \times 333 = 110,889$$

$$3,333 \times 3,333 = 11,108,889$$

$$33,333 \times 33,333 = \rule{3cm}{0.4pt}$$

THINK ABOUT IT!

Line up the place values in the products. (In other words, put all the ones in the same column.)

BIG FAT HINT • Place a 0 in front of the first 9 (09). • The answer is more than a billion (1,000,000,000).

Triple Play 2

What is 3,334 × 3,334? Study this number pattern to find the answer.
Then continue the pattern one more time. No calculators are allowed.

$$4 \times 4 = 16$$

$$34 \times 34 = 1{,}156$$

$$334 \times 334 = 111{,}556$$

$$3{,}334 \times 3{,}334 = \underline{\hspace{4cm}}$$

$$33{,}334 \times 33{,}334 = \underline{\hspace{5cm}}$$

THINK ABOUT IT!

Line up the place values in the answers.
(In other words, put all the ones in the same column.)

BIG FAT HINT The first answer
is more than 10 million (10,000,000).

Triple Play 3

What is 3,335 × 3,335? Study this number pattern to find the answer.
Then continue the pattern one more time. No calculators are allowed.

$$5 \times 5 = 25$$

$$35 \times 35 = 1{,}225$$

$$335 \times 335 = 112{,}225$$

$$3{,}335 \times 3{,}335 = \underline{\hspace{4cm}}$$

$$33{,}335 \times 33{,}335 = \underline{\hspace{5cm}}$$

THINK ABOUT IT!

Line up the place values in the answers. (Put all the ones in the same column.)

BIG FAT HINT The first answer is more than 10 million (10,000,000).

101 Brain-Boosting Math Puzzles   Scholastic Professional Books

Cats and Fleas

The goal of this puzzle is to switch the places of the cats and fleas. Put three cats in the first three spaces to the left. Three fleas go in the three spaces to the right. Then move the cats and fleas so that all three fleas end up on the left and all three cats on the right. The rules are simple:

↳ Fleas can travel only to the left. Cats can travel only to the right.

↳ Advance one flea or one cat to the next empty space.

↳ A cat or a flea can jump over any opposite piece into an empty space. For instance, a cat can jump over a flea to get to the next empty space.

Cats move left to the right. ☞   ☜ **Fleas move right to left.**

THINK ABOUT IT!

What are the only two possible moves to start?

✂ **Cut out the cat and flea pieces.**

BIG FAT HINT To start, move either a cat or flea and then jump it with an opposite piece.

101 Brain-Boosting Math Puzzles   Scholastic Professional Books

Logical Thinking 79

Gopher It 1

Gophers are hiding in this yard. Each gopher has a square of its own. Can you use logic to "ferret" them out? Here are the rules:

⤷ Each number tells how many gophers are hiding in the 8 spaces around each square.

⤷ Squares with numbers don't have any gophers.

⤷ Cross out squares that you can eliminate. For example, you can cross out all the empty squares next to a 0.

Practice Puzzle: 3 Gophers

1		2	
		3	
	0	1	
		1	

Cross out all the spaces around the 0.

1	Ⓖ	2	
✗	✗	3	
✗	0	1	
✗	✗	1	

There's only one empty space next to the 1 in the corner. It must be a gopher!

1	Ⓖ	2	
✗	✗	3	
✗	0	1	
✗	✗	1	✗

The other two gophers must be next to the 3. Cross out the space in the lower right corner.

1	Ⓖ	2	
✗	✗	3	
✗	0	1	Ⓖ
✗	✗	1	✗

There's only one space next to the bottom 1. It must be a gopher!

1	Ⓖ	2	Ⓖ
✗	✗	3	✗
✗	0	1	Ⓖ
✗	✗	1	✗

Cross out the empty space next to the 1. (Do you see why?) The third gopher goes in the last space

Now you try it!

Ten gophers are hiding in this yard.

		1					
	1	1	1	2	1	3	2
1				0			
		1			1		
1	1		0		1		0
	1				2		
	2	1	1	1			1
	2			0		1	

THINK ABOUT IT!

⤷ Use logic to fill in the spaces. For example, if only one space around a 1 is empty, then that space must have a gopher.

⤷ Use logic to narrow down your choices.

Note to Teachers: Some students may be familiar with a popular computer version of this game called "Minesweeper." Encourage them to share their strategies.

BIG FAT HINT
• There's 1 gopher in the upper left corner.
• Remember—there are only 10 gophers. Use this fact to help you place the last 1 or 2 gophers.
• If you get stuck in one area, move on to another area.

101 Brain-Boosting Math Puzzles Scholastic Professional Books

Gopher It 2

Ten gophers are hiding in this yard. Each gopher has its own square. Use logic to "ferret" them out. Here are the rules:

↳ Each number tells how many gophers are hiding in the 8 spaces around each square. For example, 3 gophers are hiding around this square shown at right

↳ Squares with numbers don't have any gophers.

↳ Cross out squares as you eliminate them.

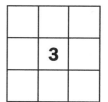

	3	

1		1		1			
1					0		
	1	2	2	2	1		
	1						1
	2	1		2	2		
	2		1			2	1
				3		1	
0			3			0	

THINK ABOUT IT!

↳ Use logic to fill in the spaces. For example, if only one space around a 1 is empty, then that space must have a gopher.

↳ Use logic to narrow down your choices.

BIG FAT HINT There are no gophers in the top row.

Gopher It 3

Ten gophers are hiding in this yard. Use logic to "ferret" them out. Follow these rules:

↳ The numbers tell how many gophers are hiding in the 8 spaces around the square. For example, 3 gophers are hiding around the square at right.

	3	

↳ Squares with numbers don't contain gophers.

↳ Cross out squares as you rule them out.

1		2		1			1
		2			1		
	1	2		2	2		1
0		2		2		1	0
			4		2		
	2				1		
	2	1	3	2		0	
		0					

THINK ABOUT IT!

↳ Use logic to fill in the spaces. For example, if only one space around a 1 is empty, then that space must have a gopher.

↳ Use logic to narrow down your choices.

BIG FAT HINT There are two gophers in the bottom row and one in the top row.

101 Brain-Boosting Math Puzzles Scholastic Professional Books

Mixed Message 1

What message did secret agent Ron Day Voo send to his contact, N. Cownter? To find out, fill in a four-letter word in each row of the puzzle. Use only these letters: *E, I, M,* and *T*. The clues tell you how many times certain letters appear in a row or column. The letters in the last column spell out the message.

Example: There is one *T* and 1 *M* in the first row. There are 2 *T*'s and 2 *M*'s in the first column. The letters of the last column spell out the secret message. Two letters are given.

	2 T's, 2 M's	2 E's, 2 I's	2 T's, 2 E's	2 M's, 1 T
1 T, 1 M	I			
1 T, 1 M				
1 E, 1 I				
1 E, 1 I	E			
1 M, 2 E's				
1 M, 2 E's				

Message

THINK ABOUT IT!

↳ Use logic or words (or both) to solve this puzzle.

↳ Make a chart of the possible letters in each row and column.

↳ How many four-letter words can you make with the letters *E, I, M, T*? Make a list.

↳ Match your chart with your word list.

↳ Each word must have at least one vowel, including the first two rows.

101 Brain-Boosting Math Puzzles Scholastic Professional Books

BIG FAT HINT • Stuck? Start at the bottom and work your way up. The word in the bottom row is METE. • Other words used in puzzle include MITE, EMIT, and TEEM.

Logical Thinking **83**

Mixed Message 2

What do you call an embarrassed secret agent? To find out, fill in six five-letter words in the puzzle. Use only these four letters in the puzzle: *D, E, I,* and *R*. The clues tell you how many times certain letters appear in a row or column. For example, the first row has 2 *R's* and 1 *D*. The letters of the first column spell out the message.

	2 R's, 2 D's	2 R's, 2 I's	3 R's, 2 D's	4 E's, 2 I's	3 D's, 1 E
2R's, 1D					R
2 R's, 2 E's					
2 D's, 1 R					
2 R's, 1 D					
3 E's					
2 D's					

Message

THINK ABOUT IT!

↳ Make a chart of the possible letters in each row and column.

↳ How many five-letter words can you make with the letters *E, I, D, R?*

↳ Match your chart with your word list.

BIG FAT HINT The word in the fourth row is DIRER, which means "more desperate." Other words in the chart include ERRED and REDID.

101 Brain-Boosting Math Puzzles Scholastic Professional Books

Figure It (Out) Skaters

Three figure skaters are named Lara, Farah, and Sara. Each one can do two of these skating moves: loop jump, lutz jump, figure 8, flip jump, spiral, and sit spin. No two skaters can do the same move. Which two moves can each skater do? Use the clues below to "figure" out what the skaters can do.

1. No skater can do a move that starts with the same letter as her name.

2. No skater can do two moves that start with the same letter.

3. Sara can only do jumps.

4. The skater who can do a lutz jump can't do a flip jump or a sit spin.

	Lara	Farah	Sara
loop jump			
lutz jump			
figure 8			
flip jump			
spiral			
sit spin			

THINK ABOUT IT!

Cross out moves for each skater as you read the clues.

Siberian Tiger 1

Three endangered tigers are hiding in this forest! Can you find them quickly to protect them from hunters? The numbers on the grid tell how many tigers your scouts have spotted.

Example: The number in the center of the puzzle is 2. That means there are two tigers hiding within sight of this center point. The tigers could be on any of the eight horizontal, vertical, or diagonal lines that radiate from the point. To find out which lines, study the numbers from the other scouts.

There is only one possible answer. When you think you have it, check each scout's number one by one. Does each number match the number of tigers that are in the line of sight?

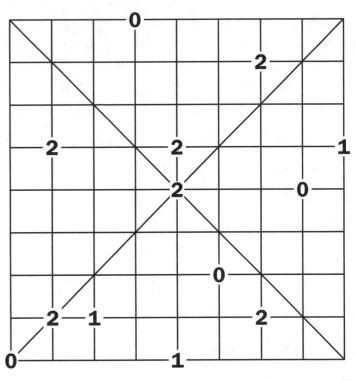

Need a warm-up?
Try the easier practice puzzle first.

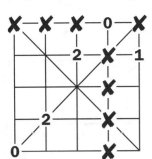

The first 0 means there are no tigers in the top row or in the column below the 0. Cross out points on these lines.

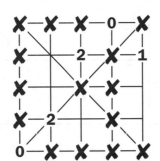

Also cross out the points along the sightlines of the second 0. Five spaces are left.

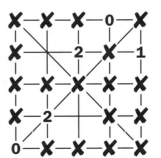

Both tigers must be in the sightline of the top 2. Cross out the points not in sight of this number.

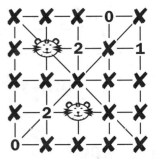

There are only two spaces left. The tigers must be there!

THINK ABOUT IT!

⤷ Which rows and columns can you rule out right away? Cross them out.

⤷ Which points are the most likely places a tiger is hiding? (Hint: Which points are visible by two number 2 scouts?) Write a ? at these points. How can you narrow down these choices?

BIG FAT HINT The tigers can't see each other.

101 Brain-Boosting Math Puzzles   Scholastic Professional Books

Name _____ Date _____

Siberian Tiger 2

Three endangered tigers are hiding in this forest! Can you find them and save them from hunters? The numbers on the grid tell you how many tigers your scouts have spotted.

Example: The number in the center of the puzzle is 2. This means that there are two tigers hiding within sight of this center point. They could be on any of the eight lines that radiate from the point.

There is only one possible answer. When you think you have it, check each scout space one by one. Make sure each number matches the number of tigers that are in the line of sight.

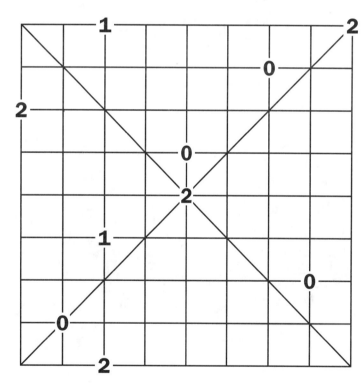

THINK ABOUT IT!

⤷ Which rows and columns can you rule out right away? Cross them out.

⤷ Which points are the most likely places a tiger is hiding? Hint: Which points are visible by more than one number 2 scout? Write a ? at these points.

⤷ How can you narrow down the choices?

101 Brain-Boosting Math Puzzles Scholastic Professional Books

Beastie Balance

You never know what a beastie will weigh—until you weigh some beasties.

↳ The first scale shows that a Glorg weighs the same as a Blorb.

↳ The second scale shows that a Glorg weighs the same as a Slork and a Plorp together.

↳ The third scale shows that three Plorps weigh the same as two Blorbs.

Now it's your turn. How many Slorks will balance a Glorg?

THINK ABOUT IT!

↳ You can solve this puzzle by guessing and checking. Plug in numbers for the Beasties until the equations balance.

↳ Another way is to substitute Beasties of equal weights on the scales. For example, the first scale shows that a Glorg equals a Blorb: $G = B$. The second scale tells you that a Glorg also equals a Slork and a Plorp: $G = S + P$. This means that a Blorb equals a Slork and a Plorp: $B = S + P$. Do you see why?

101 Brain-Boosting Math Puzzles   Scholastic Professional Books

BIG FAT HINT Plug in the number 3 for both a Glorg and a Blorb. The equation for the second scale becomes 3 = Slork + Plorp.

ANSWERS

Terminator Math, page 7
1. round up **2.** zero (z + row) **3.** count backward

Dial-a-Joke 1, page 8
The lines are crossed.

Dial-a-Joke 2, page 8
Juneau who? ("D'you know who?")

Prime Target, page 9
No one has proved or disproved the prime number rule for every even number. The prime equations are $2 + 2 = 4$; $3 + 3 = 6$; $3 + 7$ or $5 + 5 = 10$; $5 + 7 = 12$ (9 is not prime); $5 + 13$ or $7 + 11 = 18$ (15 is not prime); $5 + 19$ or $7 + 17$ or $11 + 13 = 24$ (21 is not prime).

Clocking In, page 10
09:59 ($9 + 5 + 9 = 23$)

Age-Old Problem, page 10
You are 10; your cousin is 2.

Add Across 7-11, page 11
One possible answer:

	7↓				7↓	
	5	11↓	7↓		11↓	1
7→	2	1	4	7↓	1	6	←7
11→	5	1	2	3		
11→	3	2	1	5		
7→	5	2		4	2	1	←7
	2				6	
	7↑			7↑		

Add Across Anything Goes, page 12
Answers may vary. Possible answer:

	15↓	18↓	17↓		11↓	8↓
18→	9	8	1		1	3	←4
18→	6	7	5		2	5	←7
17→	3	2	4	8		
11→		6	5			
11→	2	3	1	5		
7→	3	4		3	6	8	←17
13→	7	6		2	9	7	←18
	10↑	12↑		15↑	20↑	15↑

Spotlight Addition, page 13
A = 14; B = 8; C = 6; overlap of A and C = 20.

Unlucky Triangle, page 13
Answers may vary. Possible answer: from the top clockwise, the numbers are 2, 3, 8, 0, 7, 5, 1, 6, 4.

Tri-Corner Subtraction, page 14
The numbers always eventually end up as two identical numbers (such as 2, 2) and 0.

Turtle Number Race, page 15
6, 12, 18 (numbers divisible by 6, or by both 3 and 2)

Hare Number Race, page 16
10 and 20 (numbers divisible by 10, or by both 5 and 2)

Squared Off, page 17
All the squares from 1 through 100: 1 (1×1), 4 (2×2), 9 (3×3), 16 (4×4), 25 (5×5), 36 (6×6), 49 (7×7), 64 (8×8), 81 (9×9), 100 (10×10). Notice that in each step, the colored dots actually form a square on the grid.

Try for $25, page 18
$6 (kite) + $7 (ticket) + $12 (shirt) = $25;
$2 (jump rope) + $6 (kite) + $8 (rabbit) + $9 (sandals) = $25

Every Item $1, page 19
6 coins—
0 pennies, 1 nickel, 2 dimes, 3 quarters
12 coins—
0 pennies, 7 nickels, 4 dimes, 1 quarter;
0 pennies, 4 nickels, 8 dimes, 0 quarters
16 coins—
5 pennies, 6 nickels, 4 dimes, 1 quarter;
5 pennies, 3 nickels, 8 dimes, 0 quarters;
10 pennies, 0 nickels, 4 dimes, 2 quarters;
10 pennies, 3 nickels, 0 dimes, 3 quarters
50 coins—
40 pennies, 8 nickels, 2 dimes, 0 quarters;
45 pennies, 2 nickels, 2 dimes, 1 quarter

Dollar Darts, page 20
2: \$50 + \$50
3: \$50 + \$25 + \$25
4: \$25 + \$25 + \$25 + \$25
5: \$50 + \$25 + \$10 + \$10 + \$5
6: \$25 + \$25 + \$25 + \$10 + \$10 + \$5;
\$50 + \$25 + \$10 + \$5 + \$5 + \$5;
\$50 + \$10 + \$10 + \$10 + \$10 + \$10
7: \$25 + \$25 + \$25 + \$10 + \$5 + \$5 + \$5;
\$50 + \$25 + \$5 + \$5 + \$5 + \$5 + \$5;
\$25 + \$25 + \$10 + \$10 + \$10 + \$10 + \$10;
\$50 + \$10 + \$10 + \$10 + \$10 + \$5 + \$5

Nuts!, page 21
Billy found 32 nuts (15 + 15 + 2) and ate 17. Abby found 66 nuts (32 + 32 + 2) and ate 34 (twice as many as Billy).

4, 2, 1...Contact!, page 21
All numbers end up repeating 4, 2, 1 infinitely.

Roman Square, page 22
Across: a. MCCC **e.** CXLV **f.** XVII **g.** XIII
Down: a. MCXX **b.** CXVI **c.** CLII **d.** CVII

12 Angry Numbers, page 22
Answers may vary. Possible answer:

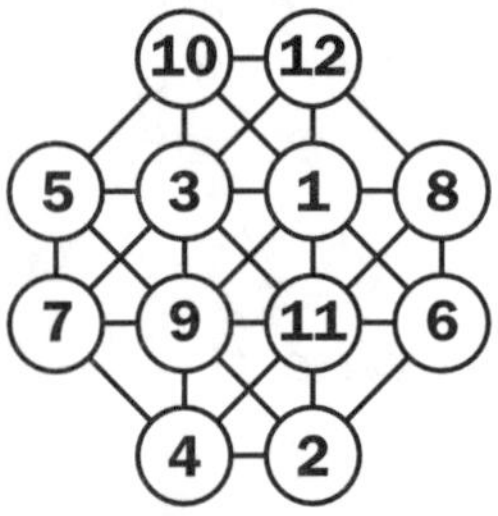

Funny Flowers, page 23
VIOLETS ON TV

Leaky Life Raft, page 24
Answers may vary. Possible answer: **Row 1—**10, 3, 8 **Row 2—**5, 7, 9 **Row 3—**6, 11, 4

Peak 48, page 25
A common mistake is to omit a number and use another number twice. Make sure students check off each number on the list. Another error is to make the bottom three numbers 4, 2, 6. In the latter case, one of the trails doesn't add up to 48 (for example, 6 + 14 + 20 = 40).

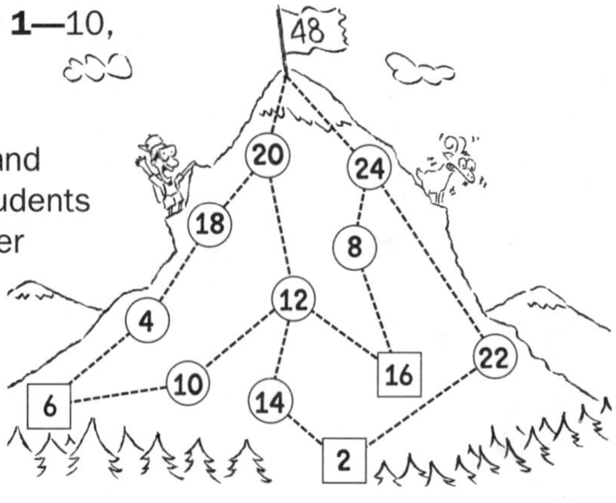

The Windy 100, page 26
The path is 2 × 5 × 5 × 2 × 1 = 100.

The Windy 500, page 27
The path is 2 × 5 (on the left) × 5 × 2 × 5 = 500.

Product of the Times 1, page 28

8		3		24
1		4		4
	2		6	12
	5		7	35
8	10	12	42	

Product of the Times 2, page 29

2			7	14
6	3			18
	8	4		32
		9	5	45
12	24	36	35	

Product of the Times 3, page 30

2			6	12
9	4			36
		8	7	56
	5	3		15
18	20	24	42	

Awe-Sum 45, page 31
2: 22 + 23
3: 14 + 15 + 16
5: 7 + 8 + 9 + 10 + 11
6: 5 + 6 + 7 + 8 + 9 + 10

7 Up, page 31
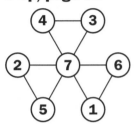

9 Up, page 32
First row: 4, 6, 8 **Second row:** 3, 2, 1
Third row: 5, 9, 7

Shell Game 1, page 33
1. $2 \times 3 = 6$ **2.** $3 + 3 = 6$ **3.** $6 - 3 = 2 + 1$
4. $6 \div 3 = 2$

Shell Game 2, page 34
1. $3 \times 3 = 9$ **2.** $9 \div 3 = 3$ **3.** $12 - 3 = 3 + 6$
4. $9 + 3 = 12$

Shell Game 3, page 35
1. $2 \times 9 = 6 \times 3$ **2.** $4 \times 6 = 2 \times 2 \times 6$
3. $12 = 6 + 3 + 3$ **4.** $9 - 3 = 6$
5. $12 = 3 \times 4$ **6.** $4 \times 2 = 12 - 4$

Fruit Bowl 1, page 36
strawberry = 1 unit; banana = 2 units; melon = 4 units; 2 melons = 8 units = 2 bananas + 4 strawberries

Fruit Bowl 2, page 36
cherry = 3 units; pear = 5 units; apple = 4 units

6-Digit Scramble 1, page 37
123,654

6-Digit Scramble 2, page 38
789,654

7–Digit Scramble, page 38
7,836,542

Dates and Places, page 39

2	0	1		1	7	7	6
0	■	9	0	2	■		0
4	1	7	■	1	8	1	2
4	5	6	7	8	■	9	
	8	■	7	5	1	2	1
1	8	4	9	■	9	9	9
0	■		6	0	1	■	6
1	9	8	4		4	0	9

Number Circle 1, page 40
Across: a. 101 **d.** 52 **e.** 96 **g.** 30 **h.** 13 **j.** 76
k. 66 **m.** 65 **o.** 60 **p.** 21 **r.** 16 **s.** 365
Down: a. 12 **b.** 0 **c.** 19 **d.** 50 **f.** 61 **g.** 366
i. 360 **j.** 7 **l.** 6 **n.** 52 **o.** 66 **q.** 13 **r.** 15 **t.** 6

Number Circle 2, page 41
Across: a. 911 **d.** 49 **e.** 24 **g.** 55 **h.** 82 **j.** 40
k. 17 **m.** 04 **o.** 52 **p.** 18 **r.** 70 **s.** 007
Down: a. 99 **b.** 1 **c.** 12 **d.** 45 **f.** 48 **g.** 500
i. 212 **j.** 4 **l.** 7 **n.** 41 **o.** 50 **q.** 80 **r.** 77 **t.** 0

Gearing Up, page 42
1. 2 revolutions **2.** 3 revolutions **3.** 4 revolutions

E.S.P. Number, page 43
6,174; if students get a different answer, have them check their math. If the math is correct, tell them to repeat steps 2 through 4 again.

Pot of Gold 1, page 44
The real pot of gold is the one nearest the leprechaun.

Pot of Gold 2, page 45
The real pot of gold is the one farthest from the leprechaun, near the northwest corner.

Escape from Antcatraz, page 46
2 south, 4 west, 2 north, 3 north, 6 east, 2 north, 1 north

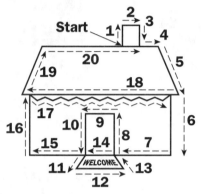

Gem Tones 1, page 47
Answers may vary. Possible answer:

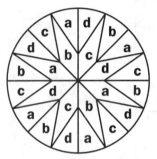

Gem Tones 2, page 47
Answers may vary. Possible answer:

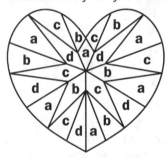

Gem Tones 3, page 48
Answers may vary. Possible answer:

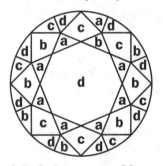

3-D Cube, page 48

Dream House, page 49
Answers may vary. Possible answer:

Letter Letter, page 49
H, I, O, X

Six Ugly Bugs, page 50
Answers may vary. Possible answer:

Creepy Crawly Corral, page 51
Note that the corrals are equal in area, even though the shapes differ.

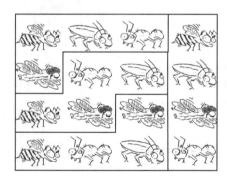

Sheepish Grid, page 52

There are 4 sheep inside the corral and 5 sheep outside the corral.

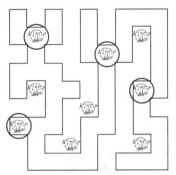

Fats Domino, page 53

Paper Door, page 54

Check students' work.

Smell the Roses, page 55

Check students' work.

Boxed In, page 56

1. 48 (8 cubes × 6 squares)

2. 24 (8 cubes × 3 stamped [outside] squares)

3. 48 total squares − 24 stamped squares = 24 plain squares

5 to 1, page 57

Chip off the Old Block 1, page 58

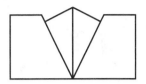

Chip off the Old Block 2, page 59

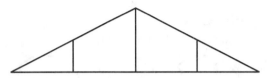

Chip off the Old Block 3, page 59

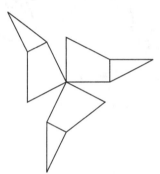

Triangle Triangle, page 60

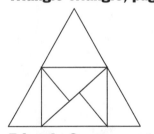

Triangle Square, page 60

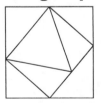

Triangle Circle, page 61

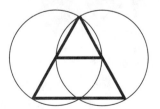

Circle 10, page 62
Check students' work.

Shell-Shocked, page 63
There are 4 whole sand dollar shells.

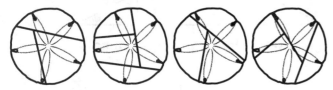

Checkered Past 1, page 64

Checkered Past 2, page 65

Even Stevens, page 66

Balanced Valance, page 67

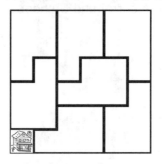

Mirror Match-Up, page 68

Victor's Vector, page 69
Unless Victor orders a course change, Easterly and Northern will crash at point B in 1 hour and 30 minutes.

31 Up, page 70
On a calendar; they are the last days of each month in order from January to December.

Strange Range, page 70
On an FM radio dial; the other numbers are AM radio frequencies.

Area Code Explosion, page 71
The middle digits of the old area codes are either 1 or 0. None of the new area codes has 1 or 0 as a middle digit.

Zip Code Geography, page 71
Zip codes get larger as you travel from east to west. Puerto Rico zip codes begin with a double zero; Pacific Island zip codes (such as Guam) begin with 96.

Secrets of the Interstates—Unlocked!, page 72

East-west interstates have even numbers, with most ending in 0. These highways also increase in value from south to north. North-south interstates have odd numbers, with the major ones ending in 5. They increase from west to east. Following this pattern, the Atlanta to Cincinnati interstate is 75.

Year to Year, page 72

2002, 2112; the years are palindromes—they read the same forward and backward.

Time Line, page 73

At these times, the minute hand and the hour hand line up.

Search in Vain, page 73

GR82CU Great to see you!

Victor's Victory, page 74

1. b **2.** c; Rotate the shape 60 degrees to the left. **3.** a; Rotate the shape 90 degrees to the left.

Victor's Victory 2, page 75

1. b **2.** a; a small, solid shape in the same relative position inside an open, larger shape of the same kind **3.** c; The line is outside the shape and the solid figure is inside the shape for all three objects in the second set.

Klepto Cat, page 76

Pocket

Klepto Cat Returns, page 76

The names of the stolen items all start with the letter *s*.

Son of Klepto Cat, page 77

Ketchup Cat shares only a tail with his father.

Triple Play 1, page 77

1,111,088,889. (Add a 1 and an 8 each time.)

Triple Play 2, page 78

11,115,556 and 1,111,155,556. (Add a 1 and a 5 each time.)

Triple Play 3, page 78

11,122,225 and 1,111,222,225. (Add a 1 and a 2 each time.)

Cats and Fleas, page 79

Answers may vary. Possible answer with 15 moves: Move Cat 3. Jump it with Flea 1. Move Flea 2. Jump Flea 2 with Cat 3. Jump Flea 1 with Cat 2. Move Cat 1. Jump Cat 1 with Flea 1. Jump Cat 2 with Flea 2. Jump Cat 3 with Flea 3. Move Cat 3. Jump Flea 3 with Cat 2. Jump Flea 2 with Cat 1. Move Flea 2. Jump Cat 1 with Flea 3. Move Cat 1.

Gopher It 1, page 80

G	1	G		G		G
	1	1	1	2	1	3	2
1				0		G
	G	1			1	
1	1		0		1		0
	1			G	2	
G	2	1	1	1		G	1
	2	G		0		1

Gopher It 2, page 81

1		1		1		
1	G			G		0
	1	2	2	2	1
	1		G			1
G	2	1		2	2	G
G	2		1		G	2	1
		G	3		1
0		G	3	G		0

Gopher It 3, page 82

1		2	G	1			1
	G	2			1	G
	1	2		2	2		1
0		2	G	2	G	1	0
	G	4		2
	2	G		G	1
	2	1	3	2		0
G		0		G

Mixed Message 1, page 83

I T E **M**
T I M **E**
M I T **E**
E M I **T**
T E E **M**
M E T **E**   MEET ME

Mixed Message 2, page 84

R I D E R
E R R E D
D R I E D
D I R E R
E E R I E
R E D I D   REDDER

Figure it (Out) Skaters, page 85

Lara: figure 8 and sit spin **Farah:** lutz and spiral
Sara: loop and flip

Siberian Tiger 1, page 86

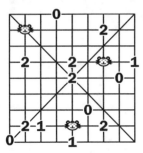

Siberian Tiger 2, page 87

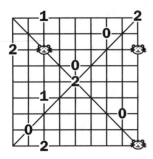

Beastie Balance, page 88

3 Slorks = 1 Glorg